HUNG JURY

*The Diary of
a Menendez Juror*

HUNG JURY

The Diary of a Menendez Juror

HAZEL THORNTON

with commentaries by
Lawrence S. Wrightsman *and* Amy J. Posey
and by
Alan W. Scheflin

TEMPLE UNIVERSITY PRESS   **PHILADELPHIA**

Temple University Press, Philadelphia 19122
Copyright © 1995 by Hazel Thornton
All rights reserved
Published 1995
Printed in the United States of America

⊗ The paper used in this book meets the requirements of the American
National Standard for Information Sciences—Permanence of Paper for
Printed Library Materials, ANSI Z39.48-1984

Text design by Kate Nichols

Library of Congress Cataloging-in-Publication Data
Thornton, Hazel.
    Hung jury : the diary of a Menendez juror / Hazel Thornton ; with
commentaries by Lawrence S. Wrightsman and Amy J. Posey and by
Alan W. Scheflin.
        p.   cm.
    Includes bibliographical references and index.
    ISBN 1-56639-393-0 (cloth) — ISBN 1-56639-394-9 (paper)
    1. Menendez, Erik, 1971—Trials, litigation, etc.   2. Menendez,
Lyle, 1968—Trials, litigation, etc.   3. Trials (Murder)—
California—Beverly Hills.   4. Parricide—California—Beverly
Hills.   5. Women jurors—California—Diaries.   I. Menendez, Erik,
1971–   .   II. Wrightsman, Lawrence S.   III. Posey, Amy J.
IV. Scheflin, Alan W.   V. Title.
KF224.M39T48   1995
364.1'523'0979493—dc20   95-24931

Contents

PEOPLE V. ERIK GALEN MENENDEZ: THE DIARY OF JUROR 9

COMMENTARIES

Foreword

Hazel Thornton

This diary is about my experience as a juror on the first Erik Menendez murder trial, held in 1993 in Van Nuys, California. Erik was tried, along with his older brother, Lyle, for killing their parents, Jose and Kitty Menendez, in their Beverly Hills home on August 20, 1989. The claim that they had been abused by their parents sparked a national "abuse excuse" debate.

The case was tried in front of two juries—one for Lyle, one for Erik—an unusual but not unprecedented method of trying two defendants for the same crime. The reason for doing this is that, while the majority of the evidence pertained to both brothers (and thus it was more expedient to present it only once to both juries), some of the evidence pertained only to Lyle or only to Erik. The goal was to prevent evidence pertaining only to one brother from unfairly influencing the verdict of the other brother. At any rate, both resulted in mistrials.

A common misperception is that the jurors who did not vote to convict the Menendez brothers of murder wanted them to go free. The fact is that every juror felt the defendants should be held accountable for the killings, and every juror made a decision as to which level of guilt they believed best fit the facts of the case: first-degree murder, second-degree murder, voluntary manslaughter, or involuntary manslaughter. The problem was not that we could not all *decide* on a verdict; it was that we just could not all *agree* on one.

The Erik Menendez jury was split evenly along gender lines, with six men voting for conviction for murder, and six women voting for conviction for manslaughter. I think it was probably a coincidence that Erik's jury was split this way and Lyle's was not. (Most of our alternates, four men and two women, say they would have voted for manslaughter.) However, I do think that men, more than women, have a hard time accepting the idea of a father sexually abusing his sons. Although both brothers complained of abuse, Lyle was supposedly abused for only a couple of years when he was very young. It was probably much easier for the men on Lyle's jury to accept or ignore this piece of evidence. Erik, on the other hand, had supposedly been abused for many years and was a physically strong young man when his father reportedly threatened him for the last time. His fear of Jose was the key to his defense; if you did not buy the sexual abuse, you had a hard time buying the fear.

Yes, the jury deliberation process was a battle of the sexes, and the men called us names, but that is not the issue here. The women on Erik's jury were not particularly compassionate or confused or controlled by their emotions. I do think, however, that because they could accept the possibility of a lifetime of abuse leading someone to kill out of fear, and *because the prosecution did not prove to them otherwise,* they were able, according to the law, to give Erik the benefit of their reasonable doubt.

As of August 1995, Los Angeles District Attorney Gil Garcetti plans to retry the brothers on the same charge. It seems to me that, since there were two juries in the first trial, they have already, in effect, been tried twice for first-degree murder. Without further evidence, a significant difference in presentation, or a reduction in charges, I would predict another hung jury. One difference already planned for the retrial is the use of only one jury for both brothers. I am not sure of the benefits of this, although I gather it was a logistical nightmare last time (it can't be money, as jurors only cost $5 a day!). I am, however, aware of a significant drawback: although I didn't get to hear any of it, there is evidently more damaging evidence against Lyle which might unfairly prejudice a nondiscriminating single jury against Erik. Ironically, by the time this case is settled, Erik and Lyle might have served enough jail time to be perceived as "walking away from it" after all.

The Diary of a Menendez *Juror*

Everyone tells me how smart I was to have kept this diary. I didn't do it to be smart—much less to have it published. I did it so I could sleep at night. As jurors we were not allowed to discuss the case with anyone during the trial. Can you imagine sitting in a courtroom day after day for five months, listening to testimony that was in turns compelling, tedious, humorous, and painful; looking at graphic crime scene photos and other evidence; and being scrutinized by reporters, attorneys, family members, and other onlookers without being able to talk to anyone about it? (Of course, everyone wants to know if we were sequestered—and the answer, thankfully, is no. I shudder to think of it.) Being single, I suppose I could have cheated and spilled my guts to my cat; instead I sat down whenever the urge struck and wrote my thoughts and feelings on paper. This would most often occur in the morning over a cup of coffee at my dining room table. The "20/20" television news magazine showed me sitting at a computer typing away, but I didn't actually obtain the computer until very late in the trial.

I believe each one of us took the responsibility of being a juror very seriously. I suppose, being an engineer and a tele-communications planner, that I also subconsciously kept the journal as a form of documentation to support whatever decision I was eventually to make. Our courtroom notes became an important part of our deliberations, but we were not allowed to take them home until the trial was over, and there was little time for reflection during testimony.

I once turned down an invitation to appear on a television talk show to discuss how stressful it is for some jurors to serve on high-profile cases. The show's producer actually used the term "post-traumatic stress syndrome" to describe the proposed topic. While I think this term is overly dramatic, I don't deny that some jurors have become ill or lost jobs or friends as a result of their service on long trials (I think everyone on our jury was sick at one point or another), and I believe the burden would have been much heavier for me had I not been able to "talk" to my journal every day.

Shortly after the trial, my brother, Kendell Thornton, introduced me to Larry Wrightsman, his colleague in the Psychology Department at the University of Kansas. Because Larry studies juries, he was interested in reading my diary. In return, he sent me a copy of his book *The American Jury on Trial,* co-authored by Saul M. Kassin (Hemisphere Publishing Corporation, 1988). I was eager to learn more about the justice system, and Larry was intrigued by my firsthand account, which supported many of his theories and contradicted others. It was his idea to write a commentary of my journal and to have them published together.

I originally rejected the idea of publishing the journal because I feared that, in order to make it appealing to the mass market, I would have to make it much longer, adding a lot of gory details about the crime and gossip about my fellow jurors. Also, because both juries—and especially the women on Erik's jury—had been so ridiculed for their failure to reach a verdict,

I felt the public would not be interested in what I had to say.
But Larry convinced me that there was an audience for my
diary, which I also came to believe as a result of my speaking
experiences. I believe the journal/commentary combination
gives my book a perspective that true-crime and tabloid-like
books simply do not have. I think there just might be some
people who realize there is more to the story of the hung jury
of *People v. Erik Galen Menendez* than the media can possibly
convey accurately. For example, more than one intelligent, relatively well-informed friend has said to me, in surprise, "You
mean Erik and Lyle have been in jail all these years? I didn't
know that!"

Dealing with the media after the trial was a real eye opener.
I can understand the public's disappointment in the lack of a
verdict (although it can't possibly be greater than my own);
however, I found the media coverage of the case to be appall-
ingly biased in favor of prosecution. I learned quickly to speak
only to reporters who had been referred to me by someone I
trusted.

The two juries in general, and the women on Erik's jury in
particular, have been ridiculed for failing to convict the Menendez brothers of first-degree murder. We have been accused of
being too compassionate, too gullible, and too confused by the
jury instructions to make a reasonable, informed decision
about the case. We have been called "Erik's Women" and "Leslie's Girls." When Alan Abrahamson of the *Los Angeles Times*
wrote that we had voted for voluntary manslaughter because
we were "so enamored with [attorney Leslie] Abramson and
her argument," I responded: "Doesn't anyone in this town understand the concepts of 'reasonable doubt' and 'burden of
proof'? . . . If this is the kind of reporting your readers have
been relying on these past six months, I doubt there is an unbiased potential juror left in the whole state."

Talk radio was the worst. Although the people who host
these shows admittedly are not reporters, and their goal is pri-

marily to entertain, I fail to see what is so entertaining about promoting a "Fry the Menendi" yard sale designed to raise money for the prosecution and referring to those who sympathize with the brothers as "bimbo sluts." (KFI can take credit for this one.) My biggest disappointment was a prominent talk show host on KABC radio who talks a lot about morality and ethics. His topic one day was the gender split on the Erik Menendez jury and what might have caused it. His theory was that the men were more concerned about justice and that the women were too compassionate. Thinking that he might be interested in talking to an actual Erik Menendez juror, I called his show. After first accusing me of merely pretending to be a juror, he expertly sidetracked me and cut me off. He didn't even want to hear what I had to say. Maybe I should have known better than to go up against a pro, but I must say I was surprised at his rudeness.

I heard the same man a year later directly blaming the Menendez juries for some recent killings of parents by their children. His argument was that the killings would not have occurred if we had convicted the Menendez brothers of first-degree murder and sentenced them to death. I seriously doubt that the children involved thought, "Hey, those Menendez guys got away with it. I think I'll kill my parents too!"

I had no desire to appear on television talk shows, only to be ripped to shreds by a hostile audience on national television. Doing "20/20" caused enough anxiety. Because the trial, including deliberations, was six months long, it is impossible to summarize our experience in a couple of "sound bites." With television you also have to worry about how you look and whether they are going to edit your comments into stupid, thoughtless statements that will guarantee ratings.

Not all media accounts of the trial have been biased or sensationalized, however. Probably the most balanced account of the case that I have seen is the 1994 Court TV documentary "The Menendez Brothers on Trial." Fortunately the media focus has changed over time, and since the *People v. Simpson* murder trial has taken center stage in 1995, from "How could you jurors be so stupid?" to "What was it like to be a juror on a high-profile trial?" There have been a lot of references lately to the instant celebrity that supposedly awaits jurors on high-profile trials. If your idea of celebrity is being chased to your car by photographers and being criticized in the press, then yes, celebrity "status" is achieved.

I have also discovered that some people actually do take this case seriously and do not treat it as a national soap opera. I have enjoyed speaking to several groups of attorneys and law students (at Yale and Princeton, to name two), who found my comments about my experiences to be both entertaining and educational.

I have also had the pleasure of staying in touch with several of my fellow jurors. I have been luckier than some in that most of my co-workers at Pacific Bell have also been jurors themselves and thus understand a good deal of what really happens during a trial. My friends and family who have not had jury duty are at least open-minded and have expressed their confidence in my ability to reason and reflect upon my experience.

Interspersed throughout the journal are several "Dear Jane" letters. Jane and I have been friends ever since we met in ninth grade and attended Borah High School together in Boise, Idaho. Although we both eventually left Boise and now live a thousand miles apart, we have kept up a regular correspondence all our adult lives. Because I was not allowed to discuss the case with anyone, I described my jury experience to Jane and answered her questions in very general terms.

Jury duty can be a fascinating and rewarding experience. I actually know people who have thrown their summonses in the trash, and I think that if fewer people did this, more would understand what really goes on during a trial and would be less judgmental when a jury returns an unpopular verdict.

So, am I glad I served on the Menendez jury? Yes, very. Would I want to do it again? Hell, no!

People v. Erik Galen Menendez: *A Summary of the Case*

This book is an account of my experience as a juror on a high-profile trial; it is neither a definitive description nor an in-depth legal analysis of the *Menendez* case. On a daily basis, I briefly summarized and commented on the testimony I felt was important. I have necessarily omitted many details—it was a five-month trial with over a hundred witnesses. I did not intend to be cryptic in my diary, nor did I write it for the world to read; there are thousands of pages of court transcripts for those who are interested in more details. Aside from a few points of clarification [in brackets], I have resisted adding to the diary with the benefit of hindsight. That said, here is my summary of the opposing sides of the case:

The Prosecution

Lyle and Erik Menendez murdered their parents for their inheritance, estimated at $14 million.

Jose Menendez, who had immigrated to the United States from Cuba as a young man, was a handsome, successful, charismatic Beverly Hills entertainment executive. He and his wife, Kitty, gave their sons, Lyle and Erik, every possible advantage: they lived in mansions, attended the best schools, drove their own sports cars, played tennis on private courts, and enjoyed exclusive country club memberships. Relatives admired and envied the Menendez family and considered it a privilege to be allowed to visit them. The boys were athletically gifted and, through the dedication of their parents, the help of extensive private coaching, and their own determination and hard work, both became nationally ranked tennis players.

Sadly, these boys were also spoiled, and one day they decided to kill their parents because they were greedy for their inheritance. First they drove to San Diego and bought shotguns (a clear sign of premeditation). Then, to establish an alibi, they made plans to meet a friend in Santa Monica two days later. On the appointed day, August 20, 1989, they burst in on their parents, who were watching TV in the family room, and shot-gunned them to death.

Lyle and Erik disposed of the guns and drove to Santa Monica as planned—too late, unfortunately, to meet their friend. They drove home and called 911, sobbing hysterically, "Somebody shot our parents!" They were questioned by police, but, luckily for them, they were not considered suspects at that time. In fact, they were allowed access to the crime scene the next day and were able surreptitiously to retrieve incriminating evidence.

For the next seven months, the Menendez brothers successfully played the innocent, grieving sons. They even went so far as to speak at two memorial services for their parents. Further evidence of premeditation includes their inordinate interest in recovering their father's will from the family computer and their postcrime spending spree.

It was not until October 31, 1989, that Erik, the younger and weaker brother, confessed the crime to his therapist, Dr. L. Jerome Oziel. Dr. Oziel was bound by client-patient privilege not to divulge Erik's tale to anyone. However, when Lyle found out what Erik had done, he became very angry and threatened Dr. Oziel. Dr. Oziel told the story to his girlfriend, Judalon Smyth, to protect himself. It was she who, on March 5, 1990, directed the police to look at gun purchase records in San Diego, which resulted in the arrest of the Menendez brothers.

The Defense

Lyle and Erik Menendez, who had been terrorized all their lives by their parents, eventually killed them out of terror, believing at that moment that their lives were in imminent danger.

The Menendez family's fairy-tale life was not all it appeared to be. Jose Menendez may have been handsome, successful, and charismatic, but he was also very domineering, intimidating, and sadistic. Kitty Menendez was a jealous drug- and alcohol-dependent woman who worshipped her husband and resented her sons. Jose and Kitty abused Lyle and Erik in every way possible—mentally, emotionally, physically, and sexually. The boys were being molded in their father's image, and, when they didn't measure up, they were punished, belittled, and pitted against each other. The family was extremely private; the boys were systematically isolated and constantly warned not to discuss family problems with others.

The Menendez brothers enjoyed material privileges, but theirs were not lives of leisure. Although both were nationally ranked in tennis, their success was the result of a grueling practice schedule that precluded other interests and activities. Jose was constantly on hand to bark orders at them and to supervise a change in coaches who were not demanding enough or who began to get too close to the boys.

One day Erik, who was eighteen and still living at home, confessed to Lyle, who was twenty-one and just home for a visit, that their father was still sexually molesting him. Lyle confronted Jose and demanded that he stop. When Jose refused, Lyle did the one thing for which Jose had always sworn he would kill them—he threatened to tell someone outside the family. After a lifetime of abuse, the boys were hypervigilant and sensitive to their parents' every word and gesture. They now became convinced that their parents were planning to kill them to prevent anyone from finding out about the abuse, and they purchased shotguns in the event that they were forced to use them in self-defense.

On Sunday night, August 20, 1989, a series of arguments between the parents and the sons escalated to the point that the boys thought, "This is it! They're going to kill us now!" So they ran and got their guns, burst in on their parents, and, in sheer panic, emptied their shotguns.

Although the brothers felt sure someone must have heard the noise and called the police no one came, so they gathered all the shotgun shells they could find, got in the car, and drove away. They threw the guns down an embankment on Mulholland Drive, disposed of their bloody clothes at a gas station dumpster, tried (unsuccessfully) to buy movie tickets to use as an alibi, and tried (again unsuccessfully) to meet a friend in Santa Monica. Upon returning home they called 911 and, in genuine distress, reported the crime as if they had just discovered it.

Lyle and Erik spent the next several months pretending they did not know who had killed their parents and genuinely grieving for them. They spent lots of money, but no more than was in keeping with their former lifestyle, for they had never been deprived of material things or spending cash. Neither of them knew much about computers, and their father had led both to believe that they had been written out of his will.

When Erik confessed his crime to Dr. Oziel on October 31, 1989, it was done to ease his guilt-ridden mind. However, the doctor did not do anything to help Erik; instead he basically blackmailed the brothers and breached their confidentiality by repeating their story to his girlfriend, Judalon Smyth. He kept her in the relationship against her will and controlled her by threatening to tell the Menendez brothers, whom she feared, that she knew all about them. When Judalon went to the police on March 5, 1990, it was not to report the Menendez brothers for killing their parents but to report Dr. Oziel for kidnapping and raping her.

On March 8, 1990, Lyle was arrested and sent to Los Angeles County Jail. Three days later, Erik voluntarily returned to California from a tennis tournament in Israel and was also arrested.

Chronology of Events

August 20, 1989
Jose and Mary Louise (Kitty) Menendez are shotgunned to death in the den of their Beverly Hills home.

August 21, 1989
Their sons, Lyle and Erik, ages twenty-one and eighteen, respectively, are questioned by the police but are not considered suspects.

October 31, 1989
Erik confesses his participation in the killings to his therapist, Dr. L. Jerome Oziel.

December 11, 1989
Dr. Oziel audiotapes a session in which he and the brothers talk about the killings.

March 5, 1990
Judalon Smyth, Dr. Oziel's girlfriend, goes to the police with information about the killings.

March 8, 1990
Police seize Dr. Oziel's audio tapes and written notes. Lyle is arrested and sent to Los Angeles County Jail.

March 11, 1990
Erik voluntarily returns to California from a tennis tournament in Israel and is also arrested.

[The brothers remain in jail for over three years while the courts decide on the admissibility of the tapes and the therapist's testimony. While in jail, Erik begins to tell his psychiatrist of the abuse he suffered from his parents as a child.]

July 20, 1993
During opening statements in the trial, the prosecution claims that the brothers killed their parents for their inheritance, estimated at $14 million. The defense claims that, after a lifetime of abuse, the brothers were convinced that their parents were about to kill them and that they killed their parents in self-defense.

[For additional trial chronology, see the diary.]

December 15, 1994
The end of closing arguments and the beginning of deliberations

January 13, 1994
After deliberating for 106 hours, Erik's jury announces a deadlock, and the judge declares a mistrial.

Final vote of Erik's jury regarding the death of Jose Menendez:

Guilty of first-degree murder	5
Guilty of second-degree murder	1
Guilty of voluntary manslaughter	6
Guilty of involuntary manslaughter	0

Final vote of Erik's jury regarding the death of Kitty Menendez:

Guilty of first-degree murder	5
Guilty of second-degree murder	3
Guilty of voluntary manslaughter	4
Guilty of involuntary manslaughter	0

Final vote of Erik's jury regarding conspiracy to commit murder:

Guilty of conspiracy to commit first-degree murder	5
Guilty of conspiracy to commit second-degree murder	1
Not guilty of either charge	6

January 25, 1994
After deliberating for 139 hours, Lyle's jury is also deadlocked, and another mistrial is declared.

Final vote of Lyle's jury regarding the death of Jose Menendez:

Guilty of first-degree murder	3
Guilty of second-degree murder	3
Guilty of voluntary manslaughter	6
Guilty of involuntary manslaughter	0

Final vote of Lyle's jury regarding the death of Kitty Menendez:

Guilty of first-degree murder	3
Guilty of second-degree murder	3
Guilty of voluntary manslaughter	5
Guilty of involuntary manslaughter	1

Final vote of Lyle's jury regarding conspiracy to commit murder:

Guilty of conspiracy to commit first-degree murder	3
Guilty of conspiracy to commit second-degree murder	3
Not guilty of either charge	6

January 26, 1994
Los Angeles District Attorney Gil Garcetti announces that the
brothers will be retried for first-degree murder.

March 11, 1995
The Menendez brothers have been in jail for five years. A plea
bargain arrangement has not been reached, and a retrial is
scheduled for later this year. Meanwhile, a new set of prosecuting attorneys has been assigned to the case; two attorneys from
the public defender's office have been assigned to represent
Lyle; and Leslie Abramson has agreed to continue representing
Erik as a court-appointed attorney.

[As the result of taxes, mortgages, losses on home and stock
sales, legal defense, and other expenses, the Menendez estate,
originally estimated at $14 million, is now worth almost
nothing.]

Trial Participants

JUDGE
Stanley Weisberg

PROSECUTING ATTORNEYS
Pamela Bozanich
Lester Kuriyama

DEFENSE ATTORNEYS FOR ERIK
Leslie Abramson
Marcia Morrissey

DEFENSE ATTORNEYS FOR LYLE
Jill Lansing
Michael Burt

REGULAR JURORS FOR ERIK'S JURY
Hazel
Tracy
Annie

Marta*
Linda
Wendy
George*
Rocky*
Phil*
Mike*
Roger*
Ben*

ALTERNATE JURORS FOR ERIK'S JURY
Betty
Olivia
Frank
Shawn
Steve*
Harold*

*Names have been changed.

PEOPLE v. ERIK GALEN MENENDEZ

The Diary of Juror 9

Jury Selection

First day of jury duty. I had heard they were calling panels for the Menendez brothers' trial, but I didn't necessarily believe it because I thought that case had been settled a long time ago. Even I knew that Lyle and Erik Menendez were the Beverly Hills teenagers who had shotgunned their parents to death in their home because they were greedy for their inheritance. When Erik Menendez walked into the courtroom, my blood went cold.

The question of the day [for prospective jurors] was: Whose companies will pay for them to be on a five-month trial? Those who passed that test (maybe 10 percent) filled out a four-page questionnaire about their knowledge of the case and their sources of information. I said I had read about it in *People* magazine at the dentist's office.

In the car on the way home I was thinking my biggest concern was where to eat lunch every day for five months. However, I was also really confused about what the charges were, had mixed feelings about whether or not I wanted to be involved, and was unsure how much, if any, control I had over that. I guess I was feeling a little overwhelmed, because I suddenly burst into tears!

THURSDAY, JULY 1, 1993

Those of us who had previously filled out the four-page questionnaires were taken into a little jury room and given thirty-six-page questionnaires about our backgrounds and our attitudes on things such as capital punishment and child abuse. As we filled them out the judge called us into the courtroom one by one and asked us about the first questionnaire. I admitted to having heard they were making a movie about this case and to having remembered that the brothers supposedly had confessed to these murders on tape to their therapist. He asked for my definition of "confession" and whether or not I thought the testimony of a therapist should be allowed in court. I said I thought it should if I were the defendant and the therapist was on my side! He and the attorneys all laughed.

TUESDAY, JULY 13, 1993

A hundred of us were on the final jury panel. The judge told us what the charges were and explained the role of the jury, which made me feel a lot more comfortable with the situation. Then there was a bomb scare, and we had to evacuate the building and stand around outside for two hours. I met three women standing there who were very friendly but also young and animated—they made me nervous! [I was thirty-six at the time.]

Judge Stanley Weisberg, I learned, was also the judge in the original, Simi Valley, Rodney King beating trial. Despite this, I have quickly come to respect him. [This was the trial that sparked the 1992 Los Angeles riots, in which several white police officers were acquitted in spite of videotaped evidence that they had brutally beaten a black man, Rodney King.]

The charges against Erik Menendez are: two counts of

first-degree murder (or one count of first-degree murder and one count of second-degree murder) with the special circumstances of lying in wait and conspiracy. [See December 15 for final charges.]

WEDNESDAY, JULY 14, 1993

The questions of the day were: (1) In a hypothetical case of two counts of first-degree murder with special circumstances, would you be able to weigh the evidence and determine guilt without considering punishment? (2) If you found someone guilty of such a charge and the trial entered the penalty phase, would you always vote for death? Always vote for life? Or would you weigh the "factors in mitigation" and the "factors in aggravation" and make your decision based on the law?

The law says that life imprisonment without possibility of parole is a less severe punishment than death. I said on my questionnaire that I thought this was debatable.

It seems to me that, when confronted by the judge about something or other on their questionnaires, a lot of people are saying, "Oh, I didn't mean that." Well, maybe they're just nervous, but I don't have a lot of confidence in people who are either lying or who can't understand the questions!

THURSDAY, JULY 15, 1993

I had been so sure that with one hundred people to choose from they would never get to me, but as soon as they called my name I knew I was doomed! I had already decided, because I was so ambivalent about the whole thing, not to try to influence the outcome. For example, I could have always answered yesterday's questions: (1) no, and (2) yes, but I would have had to lie. Before I knew it the jury (including me) was sworn in.

I was a little disappointed that I didn't get called up to the side bar [the side of the judge's bench, where he steps down to have private conversations]. A lot of people have been, presum-

ably to discuss the more personal items on their questionnaires.
I guess mine wasn't that interesting!

Taped a "Prime Time Live" episode about this case to
watch five months from now, when the trial is over.

FRIDAY, JULY 16, 1993

Continued "voir dire" (jury selection—everyone at work
seems to know this term, but no one's actually used it in court)
to obtain six alternates. Went through about eighty-five of the
potential jurors (venire), although to get down to two hundred
people in the first place (one hundred for each panel—there are
going to be two juries [one for each brother]), they had to go
through thousands. I had heard that telephone company people were popular jury choices, so I asked around and, sure
enough, there are four of us on this one (two Pacific Bell, one
GTE, one AT&T).

SUNDAY, JULY 18, 1993

Here is my understanding of my role as a juror at this
point: I no longer feel that I am passing judgment on anyone,
exactly. The law has already been established and is clear about
which crimes are eligible for the death penalty and which
aren't. My job in the guilt phase of the trial is simply to determine which side, prosecution or defense, has the stronger case.
I do not actually have to have an opinion about the death penalty, in fact it's probably better if I don't so that I am not concerned about punishment while trying to determine guilt. Only
if we find him guilty of all the charges and special circumstances will we have to determine punishment (during a penalty phase); otherwise it's up to the judge.

I have no idea why I was chosen. Probably because I'm just
so darned reasonable and open-minded! For example, on my
questionnaire I said that I definitely thought it was possible for
a teenage boy to be sexually abused, and I agreed it would be
hard for him to talk about, just like it would be for anyone

else. However, I also said I thought it was more likely he would lie about it the older he was, and that, although parental abuse definitely has an effect on a kid's behavior, I think kids should take responsibility for their own lives at some point and not blame their parents for everything.

I also said no, I don't have a strong opinion on the death penalty, but I do think that since we have one, we should use it!

Started reading *Compelling Evidence* by Steve Martini and had to put it down again because it starts right out with a gas chamber death scene.

MONDAY, JULY 19, 1993

Last day at work. It's interesting the reactions people are having to my news, ranging from "Congratulations, that's quite an honor," and "You'll enjoy the experience," to "Oh, that's terrible! I'm so sorry." As far as my work goes, this is a pretty good time for something like this to happen. There are some projects I will still be able to work on in my spare time, like my ITP [Integrated Technology Plan], and Don [my boss] will supervise the clerks for me. Paula [a co-worker] reads two newspapers every day and is clipping articles for me to read when this is all over.

Opening Statements

There was increased security at the courthouse starting today, supposedly due to this particular trial. I was busted by the new X-ray machine for the little pocketknife I carry in my purse. They don't allow knitting needles or scissors either.

Opening statements were as riveting as anything I've seen on TV. I was glued to the edge of my seat. I think I forgot to breathe for an hour and a half! Prosecuting attorney Lester Kuriyama didn't have anything surprising to say. His comments were brief and to the point about how cold and calculating and greedy he intended to prove the defendants were. But defense attorney Leslie Abramson spelled it right out, saying, "The question isn't *who* murdered Jose and Mary Menendez, but *why* they were murdered." She proceeded to give us quite a detailed description of the years of mental, emotional, physical, and sexual abuse supposedly suffered by the boys (especially Erik, because we are Erik's jury—we were not allowed to hear Lyle's opening statements) for so many years that they felt they had no alternative in the end but to kill their parents in "self-defense."

Erik cried, noticeably but unobtrusively, when Ms. Abramson talked about his mother. Her given name is Mary Louise, but everyone called her Kitty.

The Prosecution's Case

TUESDAY, JULY 20, 1993

Today's witnesses: The 911 dispatcher who received Lyle's report of having found his parents dead on Sunday night, August 20, 1989 (listened to tape recording); the nervous neighbor who testified to having heard what sounded to her at the time like Chinese firecrackers popping; the Beverly Hills police officer who was on patrol that night and responded to the 911 dispatch.

Someone who had just returned from a trip to France said this story is big there, so I wrote a letter to M and Mme Cortes [my friends in Aix-en-Provence], who watch the evening news religiously.

WEDNESDAY, JULY 21, 1993

The BHPD [Beverly Hills Police Department] sergeant who conducted the search of the house reported having found two dead bodies in the family room and two rifles in a bedroom closet with mirrored doors. Four years ago he evidently said it was the master bedroom; now he can't remember. Another bedroom and the guest house looked, to the defense attorney, "ransacked."

A hunky Marina del Rey boat operator took the family on a charter shark fishing trip the day before the murders. The prosecution tried to establish the normalcy of the trip; the defense emphasized the noninteraction of family members. The best times to go shark fishing are 6 p.m. and 4 a.m. I have the feeling I'm going to learn a lot of trivia here.

A criminologist from the LA Sheriff Department brought a pair of bloodstained women's tennis shoes to court. I have no idea what the prosecution's point was, but the defense noted that the blood couldn't be typed due to age and poor preservation.

Detective Zoeller (he's there every day sitting at the counsel table) was in charge of the investigation and took over for patrol officers at the scene. Beverly Hills has only two homicides a year and no criminologist of its own. They showed us photos of the house and one photo of the bodies. It wasn't a pretty picture, but I saw it from a distance and I wouldn't describe it as "lurid," the way the radio report I heard on the way home did. He also talked in some detail about shotgun shells and types of "wadding" used to separate the pellets from the gunpowder.

A Beverly Hills sergeant testified to having taken Erik's statement that night (by then it was early morning, August 21, 1989). Listened to his tape-recorded statement.

THURSDAY, JULY 22, 1993

The sergeant again, this time with Lyle's tape-recorded statement, which was much longer than Erik's because he was much less distraught at the time. The sergeant, a sincere Dennis Weaver type (we are casting the movie as we go along), didn't suspect them at the time—their emotions seemed genuine to him. The excitement of the day was when the prosecution asked the sergeant if he was aware that Erik was "an aspiring actor." There were lots of objections and a couple of recesses, but the judge let the testimony stand.

I can see we are going to be getting a lot of information, and it is hard to tell now what is going to end up being important.

They didn't need the juries today, which is a good thing because I came down with a cold and was sick in bed for three days. They had hearings today, which I didn't realize until later involved testimony from upcoming witnesses and decisions as to what the jury would be allowed to hear.

Went ahead and read *Compelling Evidence*—it was just like being on jury duty and actually helped me to understand a few things, like what a grand jury is for (to determine whether or not there is enough evidence to warrant a trial).

According to Tracy, a fellow juror who works in a bookstore, the white-haired gentleman who shows up every day wearing the "Dominick Dunne" name tag is a "true-crime" writer. Fred [my television news reporter friend] asked if I'd seen Art Rascon from KABC or the correspondent from "Good Morning America." I had seen their trucks outside, but I also know that there is a press room somewhere nearby and that I am not seeing half the people who are watching the trial live on the video feed (courtesy of Pacific Bell), which is set up to avoid showing the jury. There is a section reserved for relatives and reporters; when both juries are present there are only seats for nine general spectators. I have heard they start lining up at 4 a.m.—first come, first served.

Craig Cignarelli, Erik's best tennis buddy from Calabasas High School, testified in front of our jury only. He went off to UCSB [University of California at Santa Barbara] the same year that Erik moved to Beverly Hills and started BHHS [Beverly

Hills High School]. He says Erik confessed the killings to him on September 1, 1989, but it wasn't until November 29, 1989, that he wore a body wire during dinner with Erik at the Chart House in Malibu. He did not manage to extract a confession for the police. He sure is full of himself—seems like a real jerk to me. He says he studied film-making for the purpose of being able to make good campaign commercials when he runs for Senate, right after he goes to law school. He said they [he and Erik] dreamed of a "Billionaire Boys Club" (this was stricken from the record, like we can actually forget these things). He had a very selective memory, was known to play mind games with Erik, and didn't ask him *why* he'd killed his parents or anything else about it. Evidently, Drama is a required course at BHHS.

Donovan Goodreau, Lyle's best friend at one point, admitted to both juries that he had pretended to be a student at Princeton [University, where Lyle was a student] and was kicked out of Lyle's apartment when Lyle found out he had no intention of enrolling. This was presumably because Donovan would no longer have been considered a suitable friend by Lyle's controlling father. He "lost" his wallet in the move, and his ID was later used to buy the guns. He seemed completely sincere and claims to have really valued their friendship.

So far the prosecution's strategy seems to be that the side with the best-looking witnesses is going to win. We on the jury do not discuss the case among ourselves, but we do sometimes make comments about the witnesses' credibility. The tough thing is that just because you're looking at someone you wouldn't trust as far as you could throw them doesn't mean they're not telling the truth all or part of the time on the stand.

TUESDAY, JULY 27, 1993

Traded seats with the "gold" (Lyle's) jury. We are the "blue" (Erik's) jury. Judge Weisberg went to UCLA [whose colors are gold and blue]. We have to sit in the audience this week while they sit in the jury box. [We took turns throughout the trial for various reasons, including vantage point and comfort.]

Waited around a lot today. Only saw a half-hour of testimony—from the woman who sold two shotguns to Lyle and Erik at a Big 5 Sporting Goods store in San Diego. She was accused by Ms. Abramson of deducing versus actually remembering events.

The prosecution seems to be trying to prove that the boys killed their parents. I thought we'd already established that!?

Something newsworthy evidently happened in Lyle's trial today (in front of the gold jury while we waited around), but Fred successfully restrained himself on the phone about it.

WEDNESDAY, JULY 28, 1993

Worked in the morning at Pacific Bell. It seemed like I'd been gone for months instead of days. People were surprised to see me—they hadn't expected to for five months! In the afternoon we spent only twenty minutes in court—Donovan Goodreau testified that the letter he just recently received from Lyle contained no threats about his plans to testify at the trial.

THURSDAY, JULY 29, 1993

Worked all day at Pacific Bell.

FRIDAY, JULY 30, 1993

Wasn't needed in court after all so took the day off. They were having hearings today, I learned, regarding what testimony would and would not be allowed by the boys' therapist. I should think they'd have had time during the past four years to decide these things before the trial actually started.

MONDAY, AUGUST 2, 1993

A computer expert and his pregnant (at the time of the killings) wife testified today. He had been called by Carlos Menendez (cousin? uncle? I forget) to try to recover some erased files on the family computer, presumably having to do

with an updated will. The issues seemed to be the positive identification of Craig C. [Ignarelli], Erik's friend who testified earlier that he was there that day (were they influenced by having
seen him on TV?), and Erik's and Carlos's apparent attitudes
toward the files not being found (upset).

Judge Weisberg frequently asks us if we've been exposed
to any news of the trial, and we all say "no" every time (except
Frank). I have a hard time believing it though, so today I wrote
him a note describing what minimal exposure I've had, what I
mean when I say "no," and letting him decide. He apparently
doesn't have a problem with it.

In the afternoon a different computer expert testified that
Lyle had called him to come over the day before and erase the
hard drive [on the family computer] using Norton's Wipe Util-
ity. So, on the one hand, these files were not recoverable by the
other computer guy the next day, but, on the other hand, he
says there wasn't anything much in these files anyway (no will).

A woman from Slavic Jewelers (Century City Mall) said
she sold Lyle and Erik Rolex watches and money clips on August 24, 1989. They were authorized to use their father's
American Express card. She was unexplainably cranky about
the whole thing.

TUESDAY, AUGUST 3, 1993

OK, now we've had our "lurid" photographs, and plenty
of them. The deputy medical examiner for the LA County Cor-
oner's office, a forensic pathologist [Irwin Golden], described
in excruciating detail the gunshot wounds sustained by Jose
and Mary Menendez. There were many more wounds than the
physical evidence of shotgun shells accounts for. All day. He
was just as geeky and fidgety as can be.

WEDNESDAY, AUGUST 11, 1993

Today ends six consecutive days of testimony by Dr. Weasel, I mean Dr. L. (Leon) Jerome Oziel, the prosecution's star
witness. For the most part it has been very entertaining to

watch the defense team destroy his credibility. However, it got kind of ugly in the end. Yesterday both sides got down to reading embarrassing excerpts from love letters written by the Dr. and his girlfriend. The question is: Which one of the two [the doctor or the girlfriend] was obsessed with the other and was using knowledge of the murders to manipulate the other?

Ms. Abramson obviously despises the man, and I find the way he can't give a straight answer to be extremely irritating myself. He really gets her going, and today Judge Weisberg raised his voice for the first time and told her that if she couldn't ask the questions in "a more lawyerly fashion," she may not be asking any more questions at all! I found myself alone in an elevator with her right after that. I said, "Oh, hello." She smiled and growled warily, "Don't talk to me," in a way that I took to mean: (1) you know we're not supposed to talk to each other; (2) leave me alone, I'm having a bad day; and (3) under different circumstances we could go have a drink together later and blow off steam!

Oziel's basic story is that on October 31, 1989, Erik confessed to the murders during a specially scheduled therapy session. Lyle was called to join them. He was upset with Erik and was menacing toward Dr. Oziel. The Dr. sent his wife and children to stay in a hotel for a few days while he stayed with his girlfriend, Judalon Smyth. He met with the boys again on November 2, 1989, and, a week or two later, made a tape describing those two sessions, which he kept in a safe deposit box. If this is the "confession" tape I have heard about, it is not at all what I expected. [See November 17.]

Anyway, after living in the Dr.'s house for three months, out of fear or coercion (who knows?), Judalon Smyth called the police, and on March 8, 1990, they seized the tapes, among other things. So now I know why it took so long for this case to come to trial—the tapes were held up in litigation for two years. The issues are: (1) Was Dr. Oziel acting unethically when he told his girlfriend about the confession? (2) If so, how much of what he's telling us is a cover-up? (3) Was he trying to profit from the boys' inheritance?

One of Lyle's defense attorneys, Michael Burt, surprised me today. I had been thinking of him as meek and mild mannered until he went for Oziel's jugular with the following exchange:

> *Burt:* So you didn't use this situation to threaten Judalon Smyth?
>
> *Oziel:* No, I didn't.
>
> *Burt:* Are you *sure* about that? (He then played a tape-recorded conversation between Oziel and Smyth, who was wired for sound at the time, in which he definitely threatened her.)

THURSDAY, AUGUST 12, 1993

Det. Zoeller again. Listened to a boring tape of an interview with Erik in New Jersey on September 17, 1989, in which Erik suggested that Det. Zoeller talk to Dr. O.

Brad Brunon, Dr. Oziel's attorney, said he told Dr. O he could certainly go to the police with his story, but that it was doubtful they'd react with so little evidence and that it was questionable the case would find its way into the legal system.

Dr. Lulow, Dr. Oziel's therapist, said he was also Dr. O's supervisor at the time he was on probation in 1986 for gross negligence in a "dual relationship." [This is where a professional, such as a therapist, becomes personally involved with a client.] Anyway, there was a case which ruled that a psychologist has a legal obligation to warn a third party of threats made by a patient. Dr. Lulow said he told Dr. O that he felt the law would definitely apply to the therapist himself if he felt threatened and that he could therefore go to the police (he didn't, though).

FRIDAY, AUGUST 13, 1993

Mark Heffernan is the tennis coach who was hired to coach Erik exclusively after his parents' deaths. He said he helped Erik get settled in an apartment in the Marina Del Rey Towers and managed all his waking moments.

MONDAY, AUGUST 16, 1993

A woman testified to nearly having sold Lyle a $900K+, 3,000-square foot luxury penthouse condominium at the Marina Del Rey Towers. He canceled the deal within a week.

(The prosecution rests its case.)

The Defense's Case

Aunt Marta [Cano], Jose's sister, took the stand, but they got off on a tangent and decided to take her off and bring her back later. She has been in court nearly every day, and always smiles and nods supportingly at the boys.

Dr. Briere gave us what amounted to an informative seminar on child abuse. He spoke of three types of abuse: physical, sexual, and psychological. He supposedly has no knowledge of the circumstances of this case and has not examined either defendant. He seemed very calm, sincere, and knowledgeable. The prosecution mostly wanted to know if someone could lie about having been sexually abused and how difficult it would be to leave an abusive relationship. Most of the cross-examination actually benefited the defense's case! There were a lot of references to "battered women's syndrome." I wasn't sure if they were just trying to relate the two types of abuse, or if they were implying that Kitty had been abused by Jose.

TUESDAY, AUGUST 17, 1993

A male cousin of the boys who spent summers with them as children testified to some of the strict rules of the Menendez household and some of the punishments that were administered.

There has been a disconcerting change in the judge's demeanor during this new phase of the trial. He seems irritated and impatient with the defense. I wonder why?

WEDNESDAY, AUGUST 18, 1993

Two older, female cousins, sisters (Diane Vandermolen was the pregnant, more emotional one), who spent time in the Menendez household, told similar stories (one as late as 1983): showing emotion was considered a sign of weakness; no affection was shown to the boys; no crying was allowed; there were daily intellectual mealtime quizzes; competition was encouraged; losers were belittled; the boys and dad showered together after tennis (even when Lyle was age fifteen); they maintained an arduous tennis regimen; Kitty had fits, took the boys on "joy rides," and drank; Jose was dominating; no neighborhood kids ever visited; they maintained a perfect family image; etc.; etc.

Accidentally saw a TV news sound bite which corroborated my suspicion that the judge is biased against the defense, but whether it's in principle or because they've been difficult or "going too far," I'm not sure. That Abramson can be a handful!

THURSDAY, AUGUST 19, 1993

Cynthia McPhee, Dr. Oziel's ex-housekeeper, flew down from Vancouver just to say, "He's the most dishonest man I have ever known in my life." No cross-examination!

FRIDAY, AUGUST 20, 1993

A tennis coach from New Jersey, only one of several they [the boys] had at the same time, said he spent twenty hours a week with them. [The Menendez family lived in Princeton,

New Jersey, for several years before Jose, Kitty, and fifteen-year-old Erik moved to California in 1986.] They were his favorite kids. There were unpleasant debates over his coaching style versus Jose's. He only stuck with the situation as long as he did because he felt he was the only good thing the boys had in their lives. The coach got choked up, and Erik looked very sad during this testimony.

A young female lifeguard/swim coach from New Jersey said Erik was dropped off every day, rain or shine, all day, at the country club. He never talked to the other kids and seemed lonely to her. Lyle spent most of his time on the tennis courts. Jose would show up after Erik had already had a rigorous swim practice and make him swim more laps with him.

SUNDAY, AUGUST 22, 1993

Worked a lot of overtime at Pacific Bell this weekend. Found an article in [my co-worker] Sandi's *Psychology Today* magazine about why kids kill their parents and filed it away to read later.

MONDAY, AUGUST 23, 1993

Another female cousin (Marianne Cano) told the same story as the other cousins.

Marta Cano again, supportive aunt and Erik's godmother, described how the boys were treated as babies.

TUESDAY, AUGUST 24, 1993

Today Aunt Marta told stories of Kitty's neglect of the children, such as continuing to shop when the boys got lost at a shopping mall and when Erik cut his head and needed stitches.

WEDNESDAY, AUGUST 25, 1993

Marta Cano was a witness to the will (her sister Terry was executor) and filed the insurance claim for the boys after their father's death. She managed Erik's money for him and says he had no interest in it. The things he did spend money on (apartment, furniture, Jeep) were in keeping with his parents' lifestyle. The Rolexes were Lyle's idea, she says.

She spoke very convincingly of her reasons for not telling Det. Zoeller of the family's personal problems (he didn't ask; no one suspected the boys at the time; and she was trying to preserve the family's dignity), and spoke of her own integrity and desire to tell the truth. She is apparently a divorced woman who raised five kids on her own and worked her way from day-care worker to financial adviser to stockbroker.

Kuriyama: Was there anything you admired about Jose?

Marta: Yes, I admired the way he manipulated people.

A nerdy soccer coach from when Lyle was eleven to twelve years old told the same story as the other coaches.

"Mary Lou's best friend" (from before they had kids) says her family visited the Menendez home weekly for several years. Her three girls played with the two Menendez boys, but she would never leave her children alone with Kitty.

THURSDAY, AUGUST 26, 1993
Vacation day. One of the gold jury members is ill, and one of Ms. Abramson's parents is dying.

FRIDAY, AUGUST 27, 1993
Worked all day at Pacific Bell.

SATURDAY, AUGUST 28, 1993
Saw a segment of a TV show featuring kids whose parents pushed them to win at tennis. These kids felt unloved and resentful. Another segment was supposed to be about Michael Jackson [the singer] but turned out to be more about people who thrived on gossip about celebrities. Dominick Dunne and the Menendez brothers were shown briefly.

SUNDAY, AUGUST 29, 1993

Fred asked me today if I like the boys. I stumbled around for an appropriate answer, and he immediately apologized for even asking. What I couldn't tell him is this: No, I can't say that I have come to like them—I don't even know them—but I'm no longer afraid of them, and I do feel sorry for them. The situation, to me, at this point, seems hopeless. I can see how they might be driven to murder such cold, calculating, controlling parents, but that doesn't mean they should get away with it. And if they didn't learn better ways of dealing with bad situations while they were growing up, who knows what they will do next time? On the other hand, what hope is there for them if they're sent to prison for the rest of their lives? They won't learn anything there, and if they do, it won't do them any good. What a waste.

MONDAY, AUGUST 30, 1993

Another tennis coach. This time Erik was ten years old and played at least ten hours a week, more than the coach felt was necessary for a ten-year-old to be "ranked."

Two teachers from the elite Princeton Day School [PDS] testified that Lyle was an average student and that Erik had learning "differences" and didn't really belong there. They were criticized by Jose for not being good enough teachers, and, even though they told Kitty of Erik's problems and she had the resources, she did not help him. They expected their kids to be perfect, Lyle more so than Erik.

Here are some common themes from the coaches' and teachers' testimony: constant criticism, no praise for anything done right, unrealistically high expectations, belittling, winning is everything, etc., etc.

MONDAY, AUGUST 30–FRIDAY, SEPTEMBER 3, 1993

A secretary testified to Dr. Oziel's having insinuated himself into a business arrangement with her boss, who has since died. She considers Dr. O to be "very dishonest."

Worked Tuesday at Pacific Bell and had Friday afternoon off, otherwise had a full week of testimony. Another tennis coach, several PDS teachers, a couple more neighbors who heard popping sounds like firecrackers at 10 p.m., August 20, 1989. . . . Aunt Terry, Lyle's godmother who lives in New Jersey, says Kitty called everyday to check up on Lyle while he was attending Princeton [University] and expected her to spy on him and his girlfriend. The PDS teachers say they tried to notify Erik's parents of his various learning problems but they were basically ignored.

Aunt Terry's ex-husband flew in from Puerto Rico just to say that he saw Jose beat Lyle once and was thrown out of the house for trying to interfere.

Casey Whalen's testimony directly contradicted Craig Cignarelli's. Casey [another friend from Calabasas High School] says Erik was staying at his house the weekend Craig says he stayed at Erik's house. Casey remembers the computer man but not his pregnant wife. He and Craig were rivals for Erik's friendship, but Casey strikes me as being a much more sincere young man than Craig.

Casey's mom corroborated his story and reported having had a conversation with Craig about a screenplay he was writing about the murders and about all the money he was going to make as a result.

MONDAY, SEPTEMBER 6–FRIDAY, SEPTEMBER 10, 1993

Let's see—Monday was Labor Day, and I was in Boise for my brother's wedding. Tuesday I worked the morning at Pacific Bell. Wednesday we got out early (blue jury only), and Thursday I worked all day at Pacific Bell. So we did get in a few witnesses, but the only one I remember is Lyle Menendez.

Oh yeah—there was one woman who helped the Menendezes unpack into the Beverly Hills house and testified to having seen homosexual porno magazines and an eight-nozzle shower in the master bedroom. The prosecution said, "Yeah, but did you know Prince and Elton John had also rented that house?" And the defense said, "Yeah, but did you know that, more recently, the 'macho rock group U2' had rented it?"

Lyle started out by relating some pleasant memories of his childhood. He hated swimming, but he liked soccer. He was the most important thing to his father; Erik was nothing to Jose. He doesn't remember telling Diane about the sexual abuse when he was little [as she had testified].

Lyle was sexually abused by his father from ages six to eight. At age thirteen he became aware that Jose was abusing Erik and warned him to stop. Jose stopped but threatened Lyle with his life if he ever told anyone. Jose used to show them porno movies and tell them all about how "male bonding" was an important part of history (Greeks and Romans going off to war together).

Lyle was very soft-spoken and wept at key moments, like when he said yes, he had participated in killing his parents, but no, it wasn't for money, it was because "we were afraid." Also when re-creating his pleas to his father to stop raping him, to which Jose would reply that he didn't mean to hurt him, he loved him. Jose's love was very important to Lyle.

Anyway, at one point he began taking his frustrations out on his brother Erik in a sexual way (I am predicting a rash of toothbrush jokes), and this was the most painful and dramatic thing to watch of all: Lyle's public confession and apology to Erik, who of course was also in tears.

Jill Lansing, one of Lyle's defense attorneys, seems like a real classy lady to me. They couldn't have chosen a better person to present this sensitive material to us.

All I gotta say is that, if he's lying, someone really did their homework on the subject of child abuse. I was too analytical and tense and numb to actually shed tears (Tracy says I'm a Vulcan because I didn't cry at *The Joy Luck Club*), but other jurors did, and some of us went out for a drink afterward. It's like we're all going through something that no one else can relate to, and even though we can't discuss it much, we kind of like to just be together.

I swear I haven't heard anything that I feel is damaging to my objectivity, and I always turn it off right away, but, like I've said, it's hard to escape tidbits about this case on TV and radio, even if you do avoid the regular news broadcasts (I don't get the paper except for the Sunday *Times*). One radio talk show was asking callers: Do you believe the abuse story, and, if so, do you buy it as a motive for murder? Another talk show host was saying, "Jeez, how many times has your father told you 'Shut up, you dummy'?" Translation: *His* father has, and *he* hasn't been driven to murder (actually, my father has never said that to me once in my life). I saw Dominick Dunne on "GMA" ["Good Morning America"] or something—he seemed pretty skeptical ("keep in mind these boys are consummate liars") but said he's never been in a quieter courtroom than during Lyle's testimony and characterized it as "compelling."

[My friend] Jerry called to see if I was OK. Don said he wasn't sure whether to worry about me or not. He'd heard two reports—one that the testimony was emotional, and the jury was in tears; another that the testimony was more of the same, and the jury was unaffected. Which was it? Answer: it depends on who you're looking at, of course, but it seems to me like the blue jury is more visibly affected than the gold jury.

September 18, 1993

Dear Jane,

We are in the middle of an emotional phase of the trial in which Lyle Menendez, one of the defendants, is testifying. Erik ("my" defendant) is sure to be next. It's funny—my fellow jurors and I have very little in common, but this is one of those bonding experiences where, even though we can't really discuss the trial, there are days where we just want to be together. We'll walk really slowly back to our cars at the end of an intense day, or we'll all go to the same restaurant for lunch, as opposed to going in twos or threes. One day some of us went out for a drink, but I don't think that will be happening often.

I am delighted that you are interested in jury duty. It would be a lot more frustrating not to be allowed to talk about the trial if I also couldn't discuss the jury duty experience in general. I am keeping a journal outside the courtroom, but it may not address the things you are interested in, so ask away.

There are eighteen of us on the "blue" jury (twelve plus six alternates), and we are not allowed to mix with the "gold" jury. We are called that because our ID's and notebooks have blue and gold dots on them to tell us apart (blue = Erik, gold = Lyle) and so others will know not to talk to us or about the trial in front of us. One guy apparently got kicked off the gold jury for getting too friendly with us!

No, they do not supply snacks, but we immediately set up a table for ourselves with a coffeepot, and we take turns bringing in instant beverages, pastries, fruit, etc. We sit around at least half the time playing cards, reading magazines, giving each other advice, etc. It's really hard to concentrate sometimes because it is so noisy in there, but, considering there are eighteen of us crammed into a relatively small room, we get along amazingly well.

The jury room has its own bathroom (you did ask) for when we are stuck in there. We have frequent enough recesses to suit most people, but there is this one guy on the other jury who must have a medical problem because he gets up to go every time they have a side bar, and we sometimes have to wait for him. Almost every time they call us into the courtroom someone is in the bathroom, and we either have to knock on the door and yell at them, or they come out and—surprise!—we're all gone.

People wear anything they want. It seems that those who normally dress down or wear uniforms, like the postal workers and housewives, like to dress up in court. I, on the other hand, who normally wear dresses and pumps to work, am relishing the opportunity to wear jeans and sneakers. The female attorneys and court reporters give us quite a fashion show each day, and Marta can always tell us how much their outfits cost.

We do take notes in court, but we are not allowed to take our notebooks home until the very end. We all have vastly different note-taking styles, too. I write several pages a day, but am still on my first steno book, whereas some have filled two or three. The guy I sit next to only writes down the date, the names of the witnesses, and a very brief synopsis of their testimony such as: "Alleges father abused him."

Have you heard of a crime author named Dominick Dunne (I hadn't)? Well, he is there every single day, and I've heard he's writing a couple of articles for *Vanity Fair* and that, yes, it is a lucrative enough assignment to be worth his time.

There are only about a million more things I could describe, but this will have to be all for right now.

Sample Two-Week Jury Schedule [added to letter a few days later]:

Fri   9/10   Start Lyle's testimony (all day)
Mon 9/13   Lyle
Tue   9/14   Half-day in jury room wondering what's going on, other half off because Lyle's sick (telecommuted)
Wed 9/15   Half-day Lyle, other half V[acation]-day (went to library)

Thu	9/16	Jewish holiday, worked at Pacific Bell
Fri	9/17	Lyle
Mon	9/20	Lyle, start cross
Tue	9/21	"
Wed	9/22	"
Thu	9/23	"
Fri	9/24	End cross, redirect, recross, afternoon off (½ V)

TUESDAY, SEPTEMBER 21, 1993

I am paraphrasing, of course, but here is the gist of Lyle's story: Yes, there was physical, psychological and sexual abuse, although he never once used the word "abuse." There were also good times, and they enjoyed a materially privileged life. His father controlled every aspect of his life, from what he was to do and eat each day to what college he was to attend and what career he was to follow. Friendships were actively discouraged. When Lyle didn't measure up to his father's unrealistic expectations, he was belittled or punished, but that's just the way it was in his family. No one ever stood up to or contradicted Jose, especially in public. Despite the fact that he never felt like he measured up, he did feel that Jose loved him. On the other hand, he never did feel Kitty loved him, because she frequently told him how much she hated him and how the boys had ruined her life. She was chronically depressed, unpredictable, and prone to violent rages.

Anyway, by the time he was twenty-one he was out of the house, attending Princeton [University], and was relatively satisfied with his life until, one day in Beverly Hills, he had an argument with his mother during which she reached over and ripped off the hairpiece his father made him wear. Lyle was experiencing slight premature baldness, and Jose was concerned about improving his image in preparation for a political career. Erik witnessed the argument and hadn't previously had a clue about the hairpiece. Lyle was mortified. Afterward Erik went to console Lyle and confessed that Jose was still molesting him and had never stopped. Lyle was astonished and motivated to speak to Jose as he had once before at age thirteen.

The discussion did not go well. Lyle just wanted Jose to leave Erik alone and let them attend Princeton together, or UCLA, but Jose said that what he does with his son was his business, advised Lyle, "Don't throw your life away," and admonished him to forget they'd ever had that conversation. Lyle threatened to tell someone [I don't think he had a clear idea who] if Jose didn't leave Erik alone, and Jose said, "We all make choices in life—Erik's made his, and you've made yours," which, together with many other comments and events of the weekend, Lyle took to mean that his father intended to "get rid of" them to preserve his own political and social and family and business image. He hadn't thought it possible before, but became so convinced of its imminence that he and Erik went out and bought shotguns to protect themselves.

They didn't "just leave" because: (1) they didn't want to exacerbate the situation by making Jose think they'd gone off to expose him; (2) they thought Jose would be able to find them no matter where they went; (3) they didn't feel they could confide the whole truth to anyone else because they didn't feel they'd be believed, and they didn't want to ruin the family image, and it was embarrassing, and they didn't think the police could/would protect them; (4) Lyle loved his father and wanted to be part of his life. He relied heavily on him for direction and support.

So, after an argument with his parents on Sunday evening, August 20, 1989, Lyle became convinced that "this was it"— that they were about to be killed right then and there—so he and Erik ran and got their guns, burst into the den where his parents were (planning to kill their sons? watching TV? eating blueberry ice cream?), and opened fire. He denies that there was ever a plan, much less a "perfect plan," or that it had anything to do with money. He claims, in fact, to have been told by Jose earlier that year that he was out of the will anyway.

Today's X[cross]-exam by Mrs. Pamela Bozanich centered around two themes: (1) If he successfully lied to everyone for months, portraying himself as a victim, why should we believe him now? Lyle claims to have changed over the past few years. He has learned to trust people and has realized that his only chance now is to tell the truth. (2) Didn't this or that (many examples of his parents' injustices) make him angry? He admitted that some things made him angry when they occurred but that, as a kid, he was mostly just busy trying to adapt. For example, when his mom would lock him outside and he'd stay in the doghouse, he didn't feel so much angry as he did confused and embarrassed and sorry about whatever he'd done to provoke her. Also: (3) You were an adult—why didn't you just leave?

I had never really thought about the positioning of the bailiffs and the extent of their duties until Dave [the bailiff] started sitting over by the witness box. At first I thought he was just bored with his previous location, then I realized he was guarding Lyle. I think it's unlikely that Lyle would try to escape (he'd have to wait for an elevator like everyone else), so Dave must be protecting him from crazy people with unauthorized knitting needles.

WEDNESDAY, SEPTEMBER 22, 1993

Bozanich is really giving Lyle the third degree, as well she should. She forced him to look at crime scene photos, which made him extremely uncomfortable. She is all: Why didn't you leave/go to the police/refuse to go on the fishing trip (if you were so afraid)? And why did you buy the guns in San Diego/pick up the shells/lie to everyone (if you weren't trying to "get away with it")? The thing is, they were admittedly trying to cover up their involvement after the fact. They didn't want to go to jail and didn't want to have to explain everything to everybody. She wants us to believe that because they did or did not do certain logical things, that that proves they are lying now and planned the murder. But it seems to me that a person who is truly in fear of his life would probably not be thinking real clearly.

She is trying to make a black-and-white issue out of one that appears to me to be made up of many shades of gray.

Bozanich has an annoying questioning technique in which she says, sarcastically, "So then you (did such and such)?" when she knows perfectly well they didn't. I'm not sure if she's trying to trick them or merely insult them.

THURSDAY, SEPTEMBER 23, 1993

They must have made an agreement, as to the defendants' testimony, not to be objecting all the time, or there would have been tons of "asked and answered" objections. As it was, Abramson didn't even have any questions on behalf of Erik the other day. We are going over and over the details of Lyle's testimony.

One thing Bozanich keeps insisting is that the reason Lyle used his Sprint card to call Perry Berman from the Santa Monica Civic Center is so there would be a record of the call. He says he wasn't trying to establish an alibi, that he always used his Sprint card even for local calls. This is a small, but not insignificant, detail which I am taking personally; I, too, use my calling card at pay phones, even if it's only a 20-cent local call! Sure it costs more—I am paying for convenience.

We are expressly forbidden by the judge to drive from Elm Street in Beverly Hills [the Menendez home], to the Century City Mall (where they bought movie tickets), to Mulholland Drive (where they say they dumped the guns), to the Santa Monica Civic Center (where they were to meet Perry Berman), and see how long it takes! I can see why—it would have to be late on a Sunday night, and we'd have to take all the right streets and do all the same things they did for it to prove anything.

Coverage of the trial, or at least my awareness of it, has increased dramatically since Lyle took the stand. Channel 7 news: "Under tough cross-examination, Lyle Menendez admits he wasn't in any danger the night he killed his parents." Art Rascon: "Lyle essentially admits that he was clear-headed and that his life was not imminently in danger." Talk about taking things out of context! There are articles in *People* and *Vanity Fair* magazines (which, of course, are off-limits) and I heard Dominick Dunne on KABC radio just as he was signing off.

FRIDAY, SEPTEMBER 24, 1993

I did not expect the X-exam to end today, much less for redirect and recross to be finished by noon. Along with the increased coverage of the trial, the judge's admonishments have increased in their intensity: "Don't permit yourself to be exposed to anything about the trial whatsoever outside the courtroom. You are to make your decision based only on what you see and hear inside the courtroom. Don't discuss the case among yourselves or with anyone else. Don't make any final opinions until you have heard all the evidence and have received my instructions on the law." I was relieved when he started saying not to make any *final* opinions.

SATURDAY, SEPTEMBER 25, 1993

All I can say is either that boy [Lyle] is the best actor I've ever seen in my life or he's telling the utter truth, because he's sticking to his story like glue. Either way, he held up extremely well under X-exam, in my opinion. He appears to be polite and humble, yet dignified. He brings every accusation successfully back to his version of the truth and admits to a lot of things that are damaging.

The thing is, both stories, Oziel's and Lyle's, are plausible. Certainly not all the facts are in yet, but so far it comes down to this for me: Lyle appears to be telling the truth, and Oziel appears to be a liar.

I will be real curious to learn what the public's image of Dr. Oziel is. I'll bet it's pretty positive—he's the prosecution's star witness—or people wouldn't constantly be saying, "Didja hang 'em yet?"

Leslie Abramson, Erik's defense attorney, is getting a lot of attention from this trial. We like to think of her as "feisty," but I've heard people comment on what an "asshole" she is. They don't even use the word "bitch," which is more commonly used to describe strong women. I'm sure it doesn't help that the tidbits shown on the news don't include the hours and days on end where she is silent or well-behaved or acting maternally toward the defendants (I wonder how much of that is for effect?). All I know is, she's the one I'd want defending me!

MONDAY, SEPTEMBER 27, 1993

I can't believe how many mistakes I've heard the media make in the little bits of news I've been unable to avoid. For example, Channel 7 had a caption indicating that "Leslie Bozanich" was the pictured speaker. Well, I'm sorry, but it's either Leslie Abramson or Pamela Bozanich, and there's a big difference! Also the radio said, "Lyle will take the stand today. . . . Erik finished his testimony Friday" (it was just the opposite), and at the very beginning of the trial I remember hearing or seeing the name of the wrong judge used because we were using another judge's courtroom during jury selection. This has been a real lesson in trusting the media—if they can screw up little details like these, no wonder we are admonished to avoid the news.

WEDNESDAY, SEPTEMBER 29, 1993

These past three days (first three days of Erik's testimony) have been positively grueling. For one thing, Erik is far less articulate than Lyle, and it is like pulling teeth for Abramson to get him to make his point sometimes. She has been objected to for leading the witness many times (Don says they actually kept track and published the number in the newspaper). She was even objected to once, by Kuriyama, for being argumentative with Erik! I always thought it was the prosecution's job to badger the defense witness! Anyway, Erik is apparently rather dense (or, as Tracy would say, dumb as a box of rocks), and, unless it's all an act, I can see how frustrating he must be for Abramson to work with. Maybe she's just preparing him for cross-examination. I expected him to cry a lot, but there was only one real horrible outburst at the very beginning. He looks dejected most of the time. I can't see Lyle from where I am sitting, but I hear he looks awful. I figure it's either because he feels guilty and worried about his brother or because he's afraid Erik will screw up!

The worst was Tuesday afternoon, when Erik gave an excruciatingly detailed description of the sexual molestation by his dad.

Aunt Marta is back in the audience. I don't know where she was, but I kind of missed her!

THURSDAY, SEPTEMBER 30, 1993

This afternoon we started X-exam of Erik by Kuriyama. I wonder if Kuriyama has any idea what an idiot we think he is? Did he really think we'd be impressed when he asked the tennis coach, who said Jose was "barking" orders on the tennis court, "How did Jose bark? Like a dog or a ferret?" I think this was supposed to be a clever way to insult the defense (for mentioning the M's pet ferret in connection with poor housekeeping) that backfired.

FRIDAY, OCTOBER 1, 1993

This morning I heard a radio report that Erik was taking signals from Lyle yesterday in court. Give me a break. They said the judge and the lawyers "didn't seem to notice," and the example they gave was of Lyle shaking his head while Erik said yes, he supposed they did have some family videos of happy times. This must have been a real slow news day.

Erik claims that they went to the Big 5 in Santa Monica to buy handguns for protection but were told there was a two-week waiting period. They ended up buying shotguns because there was no waiting period. Anyway, the big news today is that, according to Kuriyama, Big 5 stopped selling handguns in March of 1986, three years before the killings! What this means is that Erik is lying, or is mistaken as to which store it was, or Kuriyama is full of it. I am not clear as to how we are to regard "facts" that are presented by counsel to the witness as, "Were you aware that. . . ?"

MONDAY, OCTOBER 4, 1993

Short day. Kuriyama has been grilling Erik about those last few fateful days. Erik has seemed a little sharper to me during X-exam. Maybe because the questions are more pointed and easier to answer, maybe because he's not taking his medication [Xanax, an anxiety reducer], which makes him sleepy (no joke).

One of the things Abramson did during direct was to ask Erik at one point, "You heard your brother testify about (whatever)?" "Yes." "Do you basically agree with what he said?" "Yes." I thought that was a strange way to handle it and only later realized just how many times we would be going over every minute of every day in X-exam.

Erik has explained to us over and over how it was they came to buy the guns in San Diego ("we just ended up there" sounds pretty lame at first but becomes plausible after breaking it down step-by-step) and why it was they used Donovan Goodreau's driver's license. The saga of Erik's real driver's licenses and fake/borrowed IDs is too complicated and hangs together too well for it to have been made up. One amusing element is his reason for not having a current, valid, California license of his own at the time: he didn't want to stand in that long line! Well, who can blame him for that?

TUESDAY, OCTOBER 5, 1993

Today was particularly hard on all of us. Kuriyama questioned Erik repeatedly and in exceedingly fine detail about the shooting itself. There were a record number of objections, including things like "asked and answered four times and argumentative" by Abramson, 90 percent of which were overruled. Kuriyama keeps comparing Erik's testimony to his previous statements to Det. Zoeller and to Dr. Oziel's notes which, to me, is a big waste of time, because Erik admittedly lied to them and let them believe what they wanted. Kuriyama made Erik look at pictures of his dead parents. He went over Oziel's notes line by line by line by line, and Erik told us his version of each. Erik looks like he's been horsewhipped and that's how I feel, too. I told Tracy I could only guess that Erik felt 100 times worse than me, and she said, "Well, at least he has a prescription for Xanax!"

After court there was a picketer out front with signs saying, "Judge Weisberg unfair to victims of domestic violence." I don't think it's related to this case, and, of course, we are to ignore it (if we can).

WEDNESDAY, OCTOBER 6, 1993

Today was Erik's eighth day on the stand. They were going to finish X-exam, redirect, etc., today and go on to another witness, but Kuriyama came down with the flu, and we were dismissed after lunch.

October 6, 1993

Dear Jane,

    Let's see, this must be around the twelfth week or so of the trial and we're all kind of getting on each others' nerves. "Our" defendant, Erik, has been on the stand for eight grueling days (so far).

What do we talk about since we can't discuss the trial? Well, Rocky and Shawn argue loudly about sports every single day (Shawn is twenty years old, and I gave him $5 for some bowl-a-thon on the condition that he stops yelling and promises not to get his girlfriend pregnant), but most of the rest of us talk about movies, books, Annie's latest date, whatever's in *People* magazine, etc. You know, real constructive and enlightening stuff. Today's topic of conversation is Linda's husband, who was carjacked last night. Everything I bring in—my genealogy stuff, office work, French *Reader's Digest*, etc.—generates conversation, but it gets so noisy in the jury room that I can't concentrate seriously on anything. I've often thought we could accomplish great things if we could focus all the energy in the jury room, but getting us to agree on a project would be impossible (what does that indicate about our upcoming deliberations?).

The thing about describing jury duty to you is that I don't know how representative this experience is. I know it's extremely unusual (but not a first) for there to be two juries. The reason we are both in the courtroom at the same time is that most (but not all) of the evidence pertains to both trials, and I can only speculate as to the reason for having separate trials in the first place. Probably because they are both eligible for death.

The two juries take turns sitting in the jury box, which is much more comfortable than sitting in the audience. For some reason the people on my jury like to make fun of the other jury. I don't know if it's territorial or what (they sometimes use "our" bathroom and pencil sharpener during side bars). This is not a competition or anything, but it's almost as if we were rivals. We (not me!) talk about how unattractive and what troublemakers they are, when we aren't all that much better looking and trouble-free (our Frank is forever asking the judge for time off to go fishing and to the doctor—he rarely gets it, but I guess it doesn't hurt to ask). Some of them have earned nicknames, notably "Dame Edna" and "The Pottymeister," and one woman has earned a bad reputation by wearing short, tight skirts and nasty-looking boots (she amazes even me). I wonder if and how the other jury talks about us!?

This trial is not like in the movies. There are lots of objections (I have made a whole list of the legal grounds in my notebook) that are either overruled or sustained, and there are lots of sidebars (judge/counsel discussions out of jury earshot) but no big theatrical tirades and only a few unprofessional outbursts. In fact, we feel a little cheated that the judge has never once banged his gavel and shouted, "Order in the court!" There have certainly been some emotional and painful moments during testimony, but, for the most part, it is routine examination: direct, cross, redirect, recross. . . . Sometimes we are puzzled by "hearsay" or "irrelevant" or "beyond the scope" objections. The judge's ruling seems to depend at least a little on how curious he is himself about the answer, and sometimes you can tell he would rather not allow something and is only doing it to be fair. Overall I think he is doing a remarkable job—there is no question who is in control of this courtroom.

THURSDAY, OCTOBER 7, 1993

I woke up this morning in a panic, thinking, "What, do I have a test today? No—I'm not in school. Do I have a big meeting today? No—I don't have to go to work. Then what is it? Oh yeah—the murder trial." I do not, however, dream about the trial, like some of my fellow jurors do. I think it's because I am writing this journal and getting it out of my system somewhat every day.

Kuriyama came in today, but, as the judge put it, he was spending more time in another room than he was in the courtroom, so we were dismissed again. (½ V-day)

This week's *People* magazine has an article on Leslie Abramson! I didn't read it, of course, but Don is saving it for me. Heard on a radio talk show that yesterday's topic was, "Women who are attracted to the Menendez brothers." Oh brother (pun intended)! I didn't even realize Lyle was handsome until I saw him smile one day about a month into the trial! Erik doesn't do anything for me. They are both white as a sheet from lack of sunshine. Today it [the show's topic] was, "Would you buy a house, even if you got a really good deal on it, if you knew there had been a murder committed inside?"

MONDAY, OCTOBER 11, 1993

Columbus Day—court holiday. I had wanted to get away—drive to Monterey or something, but Don scheduled an all-day staff meeting at his house, so I went. It was nice to catch up with everyone without having to do any actual work, not that I haven't been keeping up by working from home and on occasional weekends. It's kind of nice and kind of scary how slow things have been.

TUESDAY, OCTOBER 12, 1993

Erik's tenth and final day of testimony. Both Erik and Lyle were visibly relieved when he was finished. Andres (Andy) Cano, Erik's younger, adorable cousin, said Erik asked him, when they were around ten and twelve, if it was normal for fathers to give their sons "massages." Andy didn't know, because his father didn't live with him, but he kept Erik's secret.

Donovan Goodreau recounted having confessed his own abuse to Lyle in a Chinese restaurant. He assumed Lyle had had a similar experience, judging by his emotional reaction, but says Lyle did not go so far as to confess it to him. I was interested to note that a witness can testify for both sides in a trial but disappointed that he couldn't or wouldn't do more to corroborate Lyle's story.

THURSDAY, OCTOBER 14, 1993

Yesterday afternoon and this morning were particularly depressing. Dr. Anne Tyler was part of a mental health consortium which did a blind study of the Menendez family without having any idea that there was a homicide involved. She explained to us the six components of psychological maltreatment, which is the basis of all abuse: (1) terrorizing/endangering, (2) exploitation/corruption, (3) isolation, (4) degradation/humiliation, (5) denying educational and medical needs, and (6) denying emotional needs.

She described the developmental stages that a child goes through in life (ages zero to two they develop trust, ages two to six autonomy, etc.) and made the statement that there had been maltreatment of Erik by both parents in each category during each developmental phase of his life. I had no trouble, by now, believing that statement, but she didn't stop there—she gave us examples, most of which we'd heard before, by parent, by category, and by age group, and really tied it all up for Abramson in one neat see-I-told-you-he-was-fucked-up package.

The aspect of this that was sort of new to me is the way abuse affects the development of a child and how lack of development in one stage affects later stages. Basically what I got out of it was that Erik, having been psychologically maltreated to such a degree his whole life, was probably *incapable* of having *planned* his parents' murder.

Things picked up in the afternoon with Bozanich's X-exam (I love X-exam, I don't care who the witness is). She kept pointing to isolated events and saying things like, "Does driving your kids to swim practice constitute child abuse?" whereas Dr. T insisted that she was looking at *patterns* of behaviors and at the family as a "system."

FRIDAY, OCTOBER 15, 1993

The best witness today was Dr. Burgess, a sixty-something woman who has a Ph.D. in nursing, but who turned out to also have helped the FBI formulate a methodology for crime scene analysis. She was like this little Miss Marple character, testifying that the Menendez crime scene was "disorganized." This indicates a lack of planning, common in domestic homicides. There are thirty-two types of homicide, and domestic ones involve no forced entry, unmoved bodies, and a high degree of "emotionality." The indicators of disorganization in this case include the use of multiple weapons, choice of shotguns (very noisy), in a residential neighborhood (people nearby), in the summertime (windows open), and that there was random firing, mixed ammunition, and "overkill" (indicating that fear, rather than anger, was a motivator). She says the fact that they bought the guns in advance does not change her opinion that the killings were unplanned. Also, there are three stages of planning, and the fact that they picked up the shells and removed the guns from the scene are indicative of postcrime, not precrime planning.

MONDAY, OCTOBER 18, 1993

In addition to analyzing crime scenes, Dr. Burgess has studied trauma victims such as rape victims, war veterans, and abused children. They suffer similar symptoms such as fearfulness, withdrawal, and "hypervigilance." She explained, in great detail, how the body processes fear stimuli: at the first sign of danger it releases stress hormones (adrenaline); during the "fight/flight" stage instincts override rational thought unless there has been some kind of training for the situation; those who are chronically terrorized become stuck in the third, numbing phase which protects the body from pain (dissociation). Those who are chronically terrorized actually undergo a brain transformation and process fear signals differently, she says. They are constantly (unconsciously) monitoring their environment for cues of impending danger (hypervigilance) and react to less stimuli than others. For example, "Go up to your room," can mean to one kid, "Go upstairs and play with your toys and color and have fun," but to Erik it meant, "I'll be up in a minute to sexually abuse you, and if you ever tell anyone I'll kill you."

The picture I am getting is this: the cumulative events, overt and subtle, of the week prior to the killings were such that (together with Jose's actual death threats, their belief that he was capable of anything, and their never having seen anyone successfully stand up to him in their lives) the boys became convinced that their lives were in imminent danger. Whether or not they were right we will never know.

X-exam was pretty basic: couldn't a disorganized crime scene result from poor planning as easily as from lack of any planning at all? Dr. Burgess refused to differentiate between the two, and Bozanich persisted in a silly wedding-plans-gone-awry analogy. Here is Bozanich's theory: Lyle and Erik planned to kill their parents, but when they found out about the two-week waiting period [for handguns], they decided to use shotguns, even though they would be extremely noisy, because Lyle was going back to college sooner than two weeks. They tried to stage it to look like an organized crime "hit" but were sloppy and/or uninformed as to what that would look like. Dr. Burgess feels the signs of an organized crime hit are common knowledge: careful planning, use of a single small-caliber weapon, no fingerprints or other clues left behind.

It had occurred to me too, certainly, that an organized, knowledgeable person could stage a murder to look disorganized, but I don't think Lyle and Erik are that smart. Nor do I think they are stupid enough to have planned a Mafia-like "hit" that turned out so badly.

Bozanich keeps pointing to the fact that the boys escaped detection for seven months. Dr. Burgess says the whole point of the FBI methodology is that, in domestic disorganized crimes, the perpetrator is often the person who reports it, and detectives are trained to look for suspects in the immediate area. The fact that Erik and Lyle were not tested for gunshot residue and were allowed to retrieve evidence from their car basically means the police really fucked up. (Poor Det. Zoeller is just sitting there and taking it. He really seems like a nice, sincere kind of guy. I wonder how this will affect his career? Tracy and Annie in unison: "Can you say Pinkerton?") By the same token, Abramson pointed out, if someone were organized enough to wear gloves to protect from gunshot residue, they wouldn't need to worry about fingerprints on shells, now would they?

Among the things Abramson objected to today was the "disrespectful" way Bozanich kept referring to the witness as "Ma'am" instead of "Doctor."

TUESDAY, OCTOBER 19, 1993

More Dr. Burgess (blue jury only now). Turns out she's also an expert on child sexual abuse and has interviewed Erik for fifty hours. They really scored big with this one! I wonder how they find these expert witnesses anyway? She told us about how chronic abuse can affect a person to the point where they feel helpless to control anything in their life and don't see their options. She believes Erik is telling the truth about his sexual abuse based on the kind of detail he gives her, the kind of language he uses to describe it, the consistency within his own and others' stories, and with what she knows of the family dynamics.

The thing is, at this point, I believe it too, but I'm real tired of hearing about it. Plus I suspect that those on the jury who are not buying it are not going to be persuaded by more of the same.

WEDNESDAY, OCTOBER 20, 1993

Another day of X-exam of Dr. Burgess. We are interested in the fact that Bozanich is handling this in front of the blue jury and not Kuriyama, Erik's prosecuting attorney. Bozanich thinks Erik read up on child abuse in preparation for his defense. Well, that's possible, but I doubt they have a wide selection of the appropriate medical journals in the county jail library. Also, the story of the Menendez family is too elaborate and corroborated by too many different sources to have been made up, in my opinion.

However, one of the biggest sticking points of this witness's testimony is the issue of planning, and that's the whole point of this whole trial. Bozanich tried several more times, unsuccessfully, to get the Dr. to admit that just because something was poorly planned or didn't work out doesn't mean it wasn't planned (which I imagine to be legally true as well).

The Santa Monica Big 5 issue doesn't phase the Dr. in the least, because it has been demonstrated that Erik suffers from several learning disabilities including "dysnomia," a condition in which he has trouble naming things. [There is no Big 5 in the location he described, but it could have been one of a couple of other sporting goods stores in the area.] We have seen several examples of this, including mismatching cities and states where he's played tennis, and his describing a basement as being "unrugged." Apparently the best Bozanich can do in these situations is to get insulting and silly: "Does dysnomia cause a person to lie?" Regarding the neurobiological gene-recoding studies done on snails because their brains resemble the limbic system of human brains: "What did they do, scare the snails?" Her parting shot: "Doctor, have you ever heard of psychobabble?"

MONDAY, OCTOBER 25, 1993

Fred wants to know if he can have an exclusive interview with me after the verdicts are released. I have no idea how serious he is, but I told him he'd have to fight Art Rascon for it. I didn't tell him this, of course, but there is a chance I'll be elected foreperson. We may be all wrong, but there is a perception among the women on the jury that the men are not buying the defendant's story. You don't have to "discuss the case among yourselves" to figure out whether someone is sympathetic or not. Anyway, the men and women appear divided, and there are six of each. Although I am not campaigning for the job, I think some of the women might vote for me and might refuse to vote for any of the men. As for the men, I'm guessing they'll all vote for themselves. I am hoping that future evidence and/or the judge's instructions will unite us in a verdict even if there is disagreement on some of the details.

October 25, 1993

Dear Jane,

What did I say last time about the jury getting on each other's nerves? Well, it's only gotten worse, but we've just had a welcome five-day break.

It seems, coincidentally perhaps, that as soon as Erik left the stand, all the men on our jury got restless and started acting like children—tapping their pencils, popping their gum, making editorial comments during testimony, etc. If they were always that obnoxious I hadn't noticed. Maybe I'm just restless myself.

They released the Denny beating verdicts last week, and I am worried that we will have similar problems with deliberations, and everyone will think we're idiots. [Truck driver Reginald Denny was beaten nearly to death, at an intersection in south-central Los Angeles, during the 1992 riots that followed the Rodney King beating trial. The jury was lenient with his assailants, whose actions had been videotaped.] I know we can't please everyone no matter what we decide, but at least we're not in any danger of causing a riot!

This week Ben and Mike are teaching me about computers. It may be time for me to break down and buy one.

Since we are held captive in the courtroom, we have little else to do besides pay attention. We attach great significance to things that a nonjuror might not even notice: a snide remark by one of the attorneys, a subtle reprimand by the judge, a glance exchanged by the defendants, a third or fourth reference to something that has evidently been ruled off-limits.

Jury humor relies heavily on inside jokes. Any of the following is good for a laugh: "I do not recall." . . . "Did he bark like a ferret?" . . . "How do you scare a snail?" (Annie: "Show him some butter and garlic.") . . . "Ishi kitty." . . . a Mrs. Bozanich-like wrinkling of the nose . . . One day Ms. Abramson objected to the prosecution quoting from the previous day's transcripts because she didn't have a copy of it with her. The judge said, "That's OK—you probably have it memorized." Another day Dave-the-Bailiff was passing out notebooks to the jury, joking that this was serious police work he'd been specially trained for. He then turned to Det. Zoeller and said, offhandedly, "You wouldn't know anything about that." I guess you had to be there.

We speculate endlessly about the audience. The reporters are easy to spot, but it's more challenging to tell relatives and friends from neighbors, hopeful actors (they're making a movie), and Menendez brothers groupies. I think everyone should have to wear name tags.

Jury duty is like eavesdropping for a living. It is the only job I've ever had where every single one of my co-workers is at work every single day. No one is ever off sick or on vacation or away at a meeting or physically separated from me by more than ten feet, for that matter!

Tracy and Annie and I rented the movie *Twelve Angry Men* one night—why didn't anyone tell us it was about a boy accused of killing his father and that his alibi was that he was at the movies? We amused ourselves greatly by comparing that jury to ours.

Tracy, a talented but unpublished writer, has been saying all along that she doesn't want to profit from this trial. That is, until Annie said she knew someone who knew someone who works at Random House (I think) and wants to talk to her after the trial. Now all of a sudden they're collaborating—on what? A book? Who knows, but I don't think it will really happen. Of course, we were sitting in an Irish bar at the time. I'm not sure if the jury's point of view is marketable anyway.

TUESDAY, OCTOBER 26, 1993

Aunt Joan Vandermolen testified that her sister Kitty was extremely secretive. She had thought they were confidantes but had never been told about Jose's eight-year affair. She was ashamed to admit having found sexually explicit materials in Kitty's bedroom that she threw away to protect her sister's image. Aunt Pat Andersen (married to Kitty's brother Brian) said she tried several times to console the boys after they lost tennis matches in Kalamazoo but was always discouraged by Kitty.

We have heard so much about these relatives that it's almost like seeing a celebrity when they finally take the stand.

I got paranoid that people will belittle us like they do the Denny trial jury (we can't please everyone no matter what we decide) and took a little survey, for my own information, as to our level of education. As for the whole jury, thirteen out of eighteen have some college, seven of those have degrees. As for the regular jury, ten out of twelve have some college, five of those have degrees. Marta participated in the survey on the condition that I include this old Portuguese saying: "There's no bigger jackass than an educated fool."

WEDNESDAY, OCTOBER 27, 1993

Uncle Carlos Baralt (married to Jose's sister Terry) was surprisingly candid in that he would actually chuckle when recalling pranks pulled by Jose or situations where Kitty was hitting

him in futile frustration because he'd embarrassed her in public. At the same time, he disagreed with some of Jose's parent-
ing techniques and told him so a couple of times.

A doctor from MLK [Martin Luther King] Hospital [in
LA] went into great depth (pardon the expression) as to the
findings of his anal examinations of Erik and Lyle. He says
only 5–10 percent of all children he's examined who have been
sodomized show any "physical changes." Of those, 30 percent
were examined within two days. So, he didn't find any physical
evidence that Erik and Lyle had been sodomized, but neither
did he expect to. You'd be surprised at how much time it is
possible to devote to a topic such as this.

THURSDAY, OCTOBER 28, 1993
A man who worked at the Big 5 (the one in Santa Monica
on Wilshire) testified this morning but added absolutely nothing to the defense's case, in my opinion. Ed Fenno, a tennis
friend of Lyle's from Princeton, who lived with the Menendezes for a few months (1988–89), didn't add a whole lot either. I hate it when witnesses address the jury directly. (half-
day—telecommuted)

FRIDAY, OCTOBER 29, 1993
Things are winding down, and it is looking less and less
likely that we will ever get to see Dr. Oziel's girlfriend, Judalon
Smyth. We did, however, get to see one of Kitty's therapists
[Dr. Cox] and a man who worked with and disliked Jose in-
tensely.

Dr. Cox saw Kitty during the time (1987–88) when Lyle
was away at Princeton and she was obsessed with Jose and her
discovery of his eight-year affair. He says the only value the
boys had for her was to give them the appearance of being a
successful family. Divorce was "out of the question" for Kitty
and Jose because it would ruin the perfect family image that
was so important to both of them. Kitty wanted to be closer to

Jose, but Jose just wanted someone to run his household for him. He evidently started patronizing her at that point merely to prevent her from committing suicide. The Dr. felt her desire to commit suicide was as much to punish Jose as to escape her own misery. The potential effects it would have had on the boys was not important to her, he says.

Bozanich asked, "Isn't it reasonable for a woman in a twenty-five-year marriage to be depressed about the discovery of her husband's eight-year affair?" She is using the same argument to justify Kitty's suicidal feelings (depression, isolation, nowhere to go, etc.) that she finds so ludicrous when the defense uses it to explain Erik's and Lyle's states of mind. I feel like asking her: So why didn't Kitty "just leave"—she was a grown woman, wasn't she?

I don't think the prosecution has a clue how half the things they say only strengthen the boys' defense. In this case Bozanich is admitting and defending Kitty's chronic depression, which leads to emotional unavailability to her sons, which is a key element of their defense and possibly contributed ultimately to her death.

Roger Smith was VP and CFO to Jose's President and CEO of Live Entertainment during the last two years of Jose's life. Although he gave many examples of Jose's intimidating and controlling behavior, he says he himself was not intimidated. However, he was uncomfortable around Jose and had planned to resign and tell him exactly why when his contract ended (which would have been a few days after Jose's death). He also admits that some people liked Jose very much, and he credited Jose for turning the company around financially. (½ V-day)

I heard on the radio today that, coming up, there would be a report of some of the "bombs" they were going to drop on us next week (the end of the defense's case and the beginning of the prosecution's rebuttal—I wonder if they really are going to blow us away?). This was the hardest thing so far that I have had to turn off. I kept looking at my watch to see if it was over yet. I did, however, hear the part where a couple of guys were going to wear sweaters on Halloween and go as the Menendez brothers and that Erik was watching "Saturday Night Live" when they parodied the trial. He was reportedly amused (because it was four years ago and he has a sense of humor, not because he thinks murder is funny).

WEDNESDAY, NOVEMBER 10, 1993

This has been the most frustrating couple of weeks so far because we've been in limbo the whole time. They keep telling us the defense is close to resting its case, and we are anxious to get on with it and do our job as jurors. However, things keep happening: a key witness for the defense was postponed due to the fires [exacerbated by dry vegetation and strong winds, southern California was suffering its worst, most widespread rash of accidental and arson-related fires in years]; Ms. Abramson had "family matters" to attend to (I hear she's adopting a baby); Erik was sick in the hospital (something about his kidneys); etc. So every day we go in and wait around for half the day only to be released for the afternoon. (Do I go in to work? telecommute? take another half vacation day?) There is no lying about whether or not court is in session because it hits the radio news immediately! Either that, or I tell everyone at work I will not be there the next day, and plan my work accordingly, only to find a message on my answering machine that they won't be needing us in court the next day after all.

Monday (November 8) was the worst, because I'd heard Judalon Smyth was going to testify. I was so excited, only to be crushed by the news that no testimony would be given that day at all.

At this rate we will definitely go into December.

FRIDAY, NOVEMBER 12, 1993

We are back in court. Well, back in the jury room anyway. We spent a noisy, animated hour catching up with each other, only to be dismissed until after lunch. So Tracy, Annie, Betty, and I all went shopping. This was a very unusual thing for me to do—and it was kind of fun! After that we poured over mail-order catalogs for a couple of hours, until, finally, we got to hear an hour of testimony from—ta-da-a-a—Judalon Smyth! She said all the contradictory things to Oziel's testimony that I had expected, but it was all kind of anticlimactic.

MONDAY, NOVEMBER 15, 1993

A handsome doctor with a fancy name testified that he met Kitty in late 1987 after she was taken to the emergency room, having taken an overdose of Xanax (six). He saw her off and on until October 1988. He hesitated to describe Kitty as "secretive" but never did figure out from what she told him why her distress was so severe. He diagnosed her as having panic disorder (in which one suffers from anxiety attacks with physical symptoms so severe that one fears death) and personality disorder (in which one's behaviors are odd and so rigid that one cannot change them to suit the circumstances). As a psychiatrist he was not her therapist but was only treating the medical aspect of her condition (with drugs).

Back to Judalon Smyth: she has not said anything to change my opinion of Dr. Oziel (we agree that he is a slime ball), but she's no prize either. She says she had just broken off their relationship when the whole Menendez thing came up (Erik's confession), and he used it to frighten her and make her dependent on him. She was eavesdropping, at his request, during the October 31 and November 2 and subsequent sessions. What she didn't actually hear the boys say herself, he filled in for her and convinced her she'd heard. She claims that he abducted her in December 1989 because she was about to go to the police; that he drugged her, raped her, and threatened her to get her to stay; and that she "escaped" in March 1990 and went to the police for protection.

Well, I don't know how low Dr. O would stoop for $14 million, but I imagine controlling JS would be a piece of cake for a master manipulator like him. She says he thinks he's God's gift to women. We had to listen to embarrassing tapes of Oziel singing to her (everyone was amused but the judge, who looked pissed) and commenting on what a good "fit" they were sexually. Smyth credits the "Stockholm Syndrome" for her feelings toward Oziel (that's where hostages fall in love with their captors) and says her answering machine "had a mind of its own" and that's how she happens to have taped all their phone conversations (yeah, right—never mind that she's in the tape duplication business!).

TUESDAY, NOVEMBER 16, 1993

If only half of what Judalon Smyth says is true, Dr. Oziel is far more evil than I thought. Keeping her on the stand for another day has changed my opinion of her from "vindictive airhead" to "possibly victimized airhead."

Bozanich spent the better part of the day comparing Judalon's testimony of yesterday to that of July 1990. She (J) sounds like an idiot when she says she can't remember her previous testimony because she was "dissociating" at the time and that she is suffering from post-traumatic stress syndrome and that Oziel programmed her to say certain things that she now believes are untrue. Despite her little voice and her "muddled" mind and sleazy affair (she and Laurel [Oziel's wife] were friends who "often discussed sex with Oziel"!?), I am starting to believe her story.

Ironically, it really doesn't matter much what I think of her, because Oziel had already discredited himself quite well in my mind all on his own.

This afternoon was perhaps the most entertaining of the whole trial, albeit at JS's expense. When she protested, "I wouldn't want to have children that looked like Dr. Oziel," every person in the courtroom, including the judge, for once, cracked up. If he ever intended to use his gavel (if he even has one), this would have been the time. And when she accused

Mrs. Bozanich of being a liar, I thought she (B) was going to
spit nails (Tracy: "She dogged her."). Part of J's problem with
the DA's office is that she had gone to the police in the first
place to report Oziel for his crimes against *her*, not to report
the Menendez brothers for murdering their parents. Although
Smyth is evidently being protected as a witness, they have, also
evidently, refused to prosecute Oziel for rape, claiming it is too
difficult to prove.

I have decided there is no way to make a two-hour movie
about this case. It will have to be a mini-series.

WEDNESDAY, NOVEMBER 17, 1993

OK, now we've heard "THE TAPE," the *real* "confession"
tape in which Dr. Oziel recorded part of an actual session with
the boys, with their cooperation, on December 11, 1989. This
is supposedly the most damaging evidence against them, but,
in my own mind, the way things have been developed over the
past four months, it only served to strengthen their defense!
True, they never directly mentioned self-defense or abuse on
the tape, but it could be construed (and was construed by Ms.
Abramson and Dr. Burgess) that there were many allusions to
both. Neither did they ever mention that they hated their parents or felt controlled by them. They have already explained
that they didn't trust Oziel and didn't want to ever have to
admit the abuse to anyone. It probably wasn't until they were
faced with a death sentence that they finally confessed that. I
know people with less shameful secrets who would probably
rather die than tell anyone.

The taped session was very unprofessional and nonthera-
peutic, and it is very clear to me that Oziel was trying to provoke them into saying incriminating things. As Dr. Burgess
pointed out, any decent therapist would have followed up on
the many hints they (subconsciously) dropped; would have
been considerate of their feelings; would not have breached

confidentiality during the session; and would have encouraged them to confess to the authorities.

THURSDAY, NOVEMBER 18, 1993

Bozanich focused her X-exam of Dr. Burgess around two themes: (1) Is (whatever) "cognitively dissonant" (mocking Abramson) with self-defense? and (2) Your analysis of the tape is based on criticism of Oziel's techniques; does his being a bad therapist mean they didn't plan the killings? (Good point.)

George and I had a brief but interesting conversation during one of the many sidebars today—he thinks men don't trust other men because they all lie, and, conversely, he thinks that women believe everything men tell them. What I think, and consider to be more germane to the analysis of the tape, is that men tend to take things at face value, and women tend to psychoanalyze things to death (although I am a rank amateur compared to these attorneys and psychologists).

(The defense rests its case.)

Rebuttal Phase

The prosecution's rebuttal phase is, so far, just like an arcade game in which they line their witnesses up like ducks in a row and Abramson shoots them all down—blam, blam, blam—five in a row.

A big, burly guy named Detective Valentine (sounds made up, doesn't it?) says he was hired to guard Erik in New York City on August 30–31, 1989, after his parents' New Jersey funerals. He stayed in the hall outside the Heffernans' hotel room, where Erik slept, had breakfast with them the next morning, and accompanied them all in the limo to the U.S. Open, where they met Lyle and Jamie [Pisarcik, Lyle's girlfriend from late 1986 to early 1989]. On the way back to the hotel they stopped at a couple of computer stores at Erik's request. Then they took him to the airport. The implication is that Erik was interested in the computer will and knowledgeable enough to shop for software.

I wonder if anyone on the prosecution team saw this coming: Abramson says she's from Queens and apparently knows the neighborhoods and streets of NYC like the back of her hand. She really quizzed him down about routes taken, time elapsed, traffic, parking, descriptions of the people involved, etc. He looked to me like someone who would do anything for money (that is not to say he's getting paid to testify—no one's mentioned that).

A USAir security woman testified that a ticket was purchased for Erik's return flight to LA on August 31, 1989, but she can't say whether or not he was actually on that flight.

An armed security guard assigned to protect the Menendez home says she saw Erik in his bedroom with a male guest [presumably Craig C] (why don't they just say it—they think he's gay) on the morning of September 1, 1989 (when he was supposedly at Casey Whalen's). According to her written schedule, however, it could also have been another, less incriminating, day.

A pool repair man swears he was at the Menendez home the afternoon of Saturday, August 19, 1989 and overheard an argument between one or both boys and their mother and/or father. This is the kind of detail we're getting. He also swore that the tennis court fence and patio furniture locations were different than photos show and that no one was getting ready to go shark fishing [as the boat operator had testified].

The regular pool maintenance guy backs up the repair man's story except that there are enough inconsistencies that the visit may have been the previous Saturday. Once again, Abramson lives in Hancock Park [an exclusive LA neighborhood] and was able to quiz him down about his regular customers there, part of his Saturday schedule.

MONDAY, NOVEMBER 22, 1993

The morning was wasted because neither side had a witness ready to go.

Flor, the Menendez's live-in maid, November 1988– August 1989, was your stereotypical subservient, possibly illegal Hispanic woman. She denies seeing or hearing anything unusual in the M household, but then, she also admits to being a sound sleeper and to not understanding a word of English (she testified with the help of an interpreter). The defense, I'm sure, was hoping she'd heard the commotion on those Tuesday and Thursday nights in August 1989 (she was off on Sunday, August 20). She had little motive to lie except, possibly, that she wants to continue living and working in the United States!

Jamie claims to have had a conversation with Erik in which he acknowledged having realized sooner than August 1989 that his brother wore a hairpiece. This conversation occurred either late spring/early summer 1989 or maybe March/April or maybe February, she's not sure. [Attorney] Jill Lansing is a cool, classy lady—she dealt with Jamie very methodically, demonstrating that the only weekend she could have been in California was the weekend Erik and his parents were in Florida (Tracy: "Go, girl!"). She can't remember *anything* else about that trip. I don't know how she expects us to believe her. Erik looked incredulous; Lyle looked pissed off; Jamie wouldn't make eye contact with either one of them.

This may be the girlfriend that Lyle got pregnant and Jose took over, paid for an abortion, and broke them up, or was that Christie? They evidently got back together after the killings and broke up again—when he was arrested?—I don't know. This case is such a soap opera.

TUESDAY, NOVEMBER 23, 1993

I reserved judgment on Jamie until we were finished with her today and have decided in favor of "vindictive gold digger." I refuse to believe the prosecution actually tells people to lie under oath; however, it does appear to me that they either: (1) knowingly allow liars to testify; (2) are extremely gullible themselves; or (3) allow innocent people to testify without having prepared them for cross-examination. In any case it appears that they consistently underestimate the defense team's capability to rip their witnesses to shreds.

Brian Andersen, Kitty's brother, was the first relative to testify for the prosecution. He claims to have been closer to Kitty than anyone else, yet even he knew nothing about her depression, pills, panic attacks, and suicide attempt(s). He says she mentioned her "infidelity problem" with Jose to him but gave no details—"I didn't pry—if she'd wanted me to know she would have told me." Neither of them [Kitty or Brian] had told the other of their sons' learning difficulties. He made it sound like he spent all kinds of time with the Menendezes and knew them intimately, but, when it came right down to it, he admitted he hadn't seen Erik much during the several years prior to Kitty's death and hadn't paid much attention to him when they had been together. He had no idea how old Erik was or anything remotely personal about him.

Mr. Andersen seemed pretty sincere to me, as if he were telling the truth as he saw it and were in heavy denial. Ms. Abramson treated him very differently than the other rebuttal witnesses. Part of it may have been out of respect for his dead sister, but I also think she didn't want to alienate him. This was more like a therapy session than an interrogation, during which he almost had to conclude himself that he didn't know the Menendez family as well as he thought he did.

The only potentially damaging part of his testimony is that he said he saw Kitty and Jose congratulating Erik for his win in Louisville (but then, it *was* a big, important tournament) and saw them comfort him after his loss in Kalamazoo. This directly contradicts his wife Pat's testimony—another little side drama?—the truth of which even he didn't seem so sure by the time Abramson was done with him.

WEDNESDAY, NOVEMBER 24, 1993

If the prosecution doesn't come up with something irrefutable here pretty soon, there's no way I can vote for a guilty verdict. A gold juror couldn't make it today, so we were dismissed early after the blue jury heard testimony from Pat Heffernan. Now let me get this straight: Abramson already told the court that Erik's tennis coach (Mark) and his wife (Pat) would contradict the bodyguard's testimony as to events of August 30–31, 1989. Yet Pat Heffernan was called by the *prosecution*?!? The only thing I can figure is that she had a lot more to say about Erik's making and receiving phone calls from their hotel room than the judge would allow (presumably about the computer will and needing to get back to LA). Oh well, if we didn't hear it, it doesn't count. She says she didn't want to testify and considers herself to be on good terms with Erik.

THURSDAY, NOVEMBER 25, 1993

At Thanksgiving dinner I told [my friends] the Andersons [not to be confused with Kitty's family, the Andersens] what I'm most thankful for—the fact that *I'm* not on trial for anything! I think twice about everything I say and do these days, imagining how it could be misconstrued in a court of law.

SATURDAY, NOVEMBER 27, 1993

I can't believe I've had Court TV all along and didn't know it until now! It never even occurred to me to look until Abramson accused the pool man of watching reruns on the weekends. I watched just enough to realize that this trial is interspersed with several other trials and that it would be hard to tape to watch later. At least now I know who the handsome young reporter is that we see outside in front of the cameras everyday—Terry Moran of Court TV.

SUNDAY, NOVEMBER 28, 1993

Last night I dreamed I was playing tennis with the Menendez brothers.

MONDAY, NOVEMBER 29, 1993

Shawn came down with the flu over the Thanksgiving holiday, and we are going to wait a day to see if he recuperates [before resuming the trial]. Worked most of the day at Pacific

Bell. It is getting harder and harder to go in to work. Don has rearranged the work load in his group to where I am kind of between assignments until I get back. Also, there are rumors of layoffs in the near future.

TUESDAY, NOVEMBER 30, 1993

Shawn is still not well, and we are going to continue without him! Today we continued X-exam of Brian Andersen. According to Abramson, his motive to testify for the prosecution is directly related to recent developments in probate court. Apparently, if they are found guilty, the boys will not inherit the estate. Instead, their grandmother, Maria Menendez, will get everything. However, it seems that if it can be proved that Kitty survived Jose, then Brian's (and Kitty's) stepmother might inherit instead. My question is: What do you mean "survive"? Are we talking about the fact that she probably died a few *moments* after Jose? That's ridiculous!

According to Abramson, the estate is worth "less than nothing" after fees and taxes anyway. I got several other questions answered today: No, the Calabasas house [that the M's had built but not yet moved into] did not burn down in the recent "firestorm," but its value has decreased because all the houses around it burned. Yes, Pat and Brian Andersen are (evidently since—because of?—the killings) divorced.

Kitty's friend at the time of her death, who was "as close to her as anyone," says they had lunch together, played tennis, and rode horseback. Kitty was "happier than she'd ever been" that summer. She'd had her problems with Jose but was working on them and loved him very much. I think the problem is that no one knew Kitty as well as they thought they did. She seems to have forgotten about a phone call she made to Kitty on Saturday, August 19, 1989.

Marzy, Jose's secretary (and self-proclaimed "office wife") who followed him from job to job off and on for eight years (not to be confused with his mistress of eight years), liked the

guy. He was tough with others but nice to her; he was charm-
ing and handsome. "He was running a business, not a day
camp." OK, fine. To me this doesn't prove a thing. No, actually, that may have been part of the problem, that he was so
charismatic.

WEDNESDAY, DECEMBER 1, 1993

Two gold jurors out sick! Blue-jury-only testimony today.

The defense called a New York limo driver who swears he
took Erik straight to the airport (Delta terminal, *not* USAir) on
August 31, 1989. He did *not* see Lyle or Jamie or the Heffernans and did *not* go to the U.S. Open or stop at any computer
stores. I'm sorry, but he just seemed more believable than Detective Valentine. He also had the heaviest New York accent
I've ever heard. Even the judge had to ask him to clarify—when
asked if he swore to tell the truth it sounded like he said, "I
don't."

This whole thing about Delta vs. USAir, August 31 vs. September 1, Casey vs. Craig, and the computer will is driving me
crazy.

Dr. Vicary, Erik's psychiatrist in jail, answered another
question for me: Erik first mentioned sexual abuse to him (to
anyone), in August of 1990, after having been treated with
drugs for a couple of months. He was, according to Dr. V, "a
basket case" when they first met in June 1990. The sexual
abuse did not come up as an excuse for killing his parents; it
was related to his nightmares and feelings of anger toward his
mom (because she indicated she knew about the abuse all
along). I want to know at what point Abramson agreed to represent Erik.

THURSDAY, DECEMBER 2, 1993

Well now, it appears that Abramson had already agreed to
represent Erik when he confessed the abuse to Dr. Vicary, so I
wonder what she originally thought the defense was going to

be??? All I know is, win or lose, she's worth the $1 million I heard she was being paid.

According to Dr. V, Erik was borderline psychotic when they met. He says Erik *liked* being in jail because there was no pressure and no sex (not in the high-security section of the jail he was first sent to, anyway). He really resisted going public with the abuse story for many reasons: it was a shameful, humiliating personal secret; it would ruin the family image; he didn't want to lose his girlfriend; he didn't want to be an "Elephant Man"; he didn't want people to think he was a homosexual.

I couldn't care less whether or not Erik is gay—it doesn't have anything to do with whether or not he planned to kill his parents, as far as I can tell. However, I have the feeling that to certain other jurors it is a big, huge, important factor.

X-exam by Bozanich was of the usual "Do people who have been accused of murder have an incentive to lie?" (of course they do) and "How much are you being paid, Dr. Vicary?" variety.

I like Dr. V, not because I'd want to confide in him myself, but because he was very candid and admitted to things like the fact that this trial isn't making him any poorer and that he likes to control things (Erik was hard to control).

The two gold jurors are still off . . . ?

December 2, 1993

Dear Jane,

Your letter arrived at a good time. I was feeling sorry for myself, and it gave me a lift. It would be convenient to blame my current depression on the trial, but I really think it has at least as much to do with being lonely during the holidays, gift-giving anxiety, allergies, and being in limbo at work.

It's a good thing I haven't made any Christmas travel plans, because the trial may not be over by then. It is winding down, but then, it has been "winding down" for weeks now. I am going to have to be particularly careful at this point to exercise, eat right, and not get sick or stressed out.

We lost one of our alternate jurors this week—Shawn is sick with the flu, and the judge decided he couldn't wait another day for him to recover. The very next day, however, two gold jurors couldn't make it (one went into false labor—can you imagine being pregnant on a long murder trial?), and he [the judge] has been trying to schedule blue-jury-only testimony around them. Now my jury says he's biased in their favor, which is ridiculous. Our possessiveness is evidently not a secret—when the judge sent the gold jury into "our" jury room for a few minutes the other day, he added, smiling, "And don't touch anything!" He is so cool.

I never thought I'd say it, but I miss Shawn—even if he's "only an alternate" and "just a kid." I'm thinking what a waste these past few months would seem if I couldn't finish the trial.

I have been asked if I plan to write a book and become a millionaire. Well, I doubt one would necessarily follow the other, but the answer is NO. Here are my reasons: (1) When this is over, I want to get on with my life. If my journal—as is—generates some interest, fine, I can probably be bought. However, (2) I feel the only reason someone would want to buy a book written by a juror is if it gave you the inside scoop. To do that, I would have to describe my fellow jurors and their interactions in some detail. I think I could make it accurate and entertaining, but it wouldn't necessarily be flattering, and I don't want to hurt anyone. Also, (3) watching the trial has made me paranoid about making public statements. I dread saying something in print or in an interview that could be twisted so as to make me or the jury look stupid. Even worse, what if something I inadvertently said somehow jeopardized the verdict?

FRIDAY, DECEMBER 3, 1993

An eventful final day of testimony:

- Annie brought in a little tiny Christmas tree, and Det. Zoeller remarked, "Now *there's* a clue!" (as to how long we expect deliberations to last).
- The two gold jurors are still out. We proceeded without them. They are down to three alternates.
- Tensions were running high and the lawyers were reduced to, "Did not!" "Did too!" and "She's making faces"-type quibbling ("mugging").
- We were shown a "Lifestyles-of-the-Rich-and-Famous"-type videotape of the [Menendezes'] Beverly Hills neighborhood. OK, so the houses are close together. That's important information, but I want to see the grounds and *inside* the house too.
- Listened to a tape of Michael Jackson's [the talk show host] KABC radio program. Grant Walker, the pool repair man, had called in to report that the boys were rude to their parents. Michael's response was, "How kind of you to tell us."
- If I hear one more word about the nonexistent second staircase, I'm going to scream. [The layout of the house was referred to many times during the trial, and there was a lot of confusion over the names of various rooms and the fact that a second staircase appears on the floor plan.] They actually brought in the man who *built* the house to say nope, it was never built. Luckily he had some other things to contribute too, like how Lyle and Erik were asking him, a complete stranger to them who had only come by to pay his condolences, what they should do with their lives (not to mention their money)

now that their parents, and evidently their only source of direction, were dead.

- We had eight witnesses today, including some recalls. They were mostly for the purpose of discrediting previous witnesses. I am disappointed—I was hoping the trial would end a little more dramatically.
- There have been 400 + exhibits, and, according to Ben, who kept track, we have seen a total of 108 "swear-ins."
- Wendy became a grandmother twice this week!
- We celebrated Betty's birthday early because the blue jury is off next week. I haven't mentioned it before, but we have celebrated a lot of birthdays since July!

Closing Arguments

Worked all week at Pacific Bell! People kept asking me what I was doing there, because they knew the trial was in closing arguments (Lyle's trial is). Everybody gets confused about what's going on with the two brothers and their two juries.

Sandi asked me if I'd heard Lyle wore a hairpiece. I told her not only did I know he wore one, I could tell you why he wore it, when he first got it, who he was with at the time, how it is attached, how much it cost, who knew and who didn't!

MONDAY, DECEMBER 13, 1993

Kuriyama's closing statements were as dull as his opening statements were five months ago. He only made two good points: (1) The woman whose pool is serviced on Saturdays and the former Santa Monica Big 5 employee added nothing to the defense's case (I agree), and (2) I forgot his other good point. He spoke for maybe 1½ hours.

Some highlights of Abramson's closing statements:

- Erik's worst crime was yelling "shut up" to his father once.
- Kuriyama talked an awful lot about Lyle in front of Erik's jury.
- Kuriyama never did X-exam Erik about the molestation.
- The prosecution did not call any expert witnesses to refute any of the defense's psychological expert witnesses.
- Kuriyama called the defendants names; the defense never called Jose or Kitty names.
- Court TV brings out "the volunteers" (Det. Valentine, Grant Walker, Jamie Pisarsik).
- She called Det. Valentine a perjurer and says the prosecution *knew* he was lying. Plus, he contradicted another of their own witnesses (Pat Heffernan)!

Kuriyama stood right in front of a bulletin board full of gory pictures; Abramson left them up so their shock value would wear off. At one point she stuck pins in a photo of Erik's genitals to demonstrate what he claims Jose did to him as a child, speaking of shock value!

Abramson described the possible verdicts: first-degree murder, second-degree murder, voluntary manslaughter, and involuntary manslaughter. "Imperfect self-defense" involves an "unreasonable but honest belief" that your life is being threatened, in which case manslaughter would apply; "perfect self-defense" applies to reasonably thinking people and is not a crime. Most of us had heard, one way or another, that the judge had ruled out perfect self-defense (acquittal). The people at work seemed to think this would make it easier on the jury and would make me happy. Well, for all I knew it was going to be all-or-nothing, so I don't see how having several choices in between will help us decide anything.

Saw Dr. George today [a semiretired KABC weather man whom I had met previously]. It was his first day of jury duty, and he seemed pleased to see me. Roger came up to say hello too, and Dr. George obviously didn't remember having met him before.

TUESDAY, DECEMBER 14, 1993
Abramson continued her closing argument:

- Erik is a good person who did a bad thing. He doesn't want your sympathy; he wants your understanding.
- The point here is *not* that Jose and Kitty Menendez deserved to die (but they should never have had children).
- The prosecution doesn't have an explanation for why the killings happened when they did. They kept changing motives.
- If you didn't know anything else about Dr. Oziel, think of it this way: the Menendezes came to him in 1988; a year later the children killed the parents. Isn't that recommmendation enough?
- Lyle admitted to having fired both fatal head shots to the parents. There is no direct evidence that Erik killed anyone.
- Given the circumstances of his life, Erik responded *reasonably* to the situation.
- Showed us charts listing characteristics of Jose, Kitty, and Erik and lists of fear-inducing behaviors on the part of the parents.
- Would we feel differently if Erik were poor? If his name was Erika?
- A plan to defend does not equal a plan to kill.

At one point we had to take a break because one of our alternate jurors fell asleep and everyone in the courtroom noticed, first and most importantly Abramson herself! I don't think he has any idea that we were taking a break because of him. I'm glad it happened, because now, if we have to use him as an alternate and we have problems with him, he will be easier to justify getting rid of. I haven't said anything before because I don't know what will happen with this information, and I don't want to hurt anyone. Suffice it to say that we're talking about a man who isn't sure how old he is!

WEDNESDAY, DECEMBER 15, 1993

A couple more hours (around ten hours of talking over the three days), and Abramson finally finished her closing argument. You could tell she didn't want to give up the trial, her argument, the podium, and her reason for living the past 3½ years, but we all got choked up just like we were supposed to when she said she didn't want to give Erik up [to us]. Her dream, she says, is to see him walk down the street without shackles or guards.

Kuriyama gave a pathetic rebuttal argument, around an hour. He insulted our intelligence by saying we were gullible if we didn't find Erik guilty of first-degree murder and attacked Abramson for making more money than he does.

He said he'd been prevented from discussing Erik's sexuality overtly during the trial and rattled off a whole list of reasons why he thinks Erik is homosexual. He thinks Erik was able to describe sex acts from his experience with other boys, not with his father.

The charges in this case are different from what we were told in the beginning: (1) first-degree murder of Jose with special circumstances of lying-in-wait and multiple murders, (2) same for Kitty, (3) conspiracy to commit first-degree murder (overt acts: buying guns, buying ammo, calling Perry Berman to set up an alibi).

Deliberations

WEDNESDAY, DECEMBER 15, 1993

After the judge gave us his instructions on the laws that apply to this case, we were given only one task to accomplish today—choose a foreperson (the judge's word). We argued— not so much about who it should be, but about how we should go about deciding who it should be! Even though I was willing to do it myself, I was content with our choice. Phil has been probably the quietest and least offensive of any of us, plus he has a Ph.D. and runs a college math department, so maybe he knows how to run a meeting—?

Talk radio (KABC) on the way home: A former "friend" of Michael Jackson (the singer) was talking about that case [in which MJ was accused of sexually molesting a young boy], which is unfortunate but safe enough for me to be listening to, or so I thought. Suddenly it turns out the guy's also an actor up for the part of Lyle in the Menendez movie!

THURSDAY, DECEMBER 16, 1993

My worst nightmare has come to pass. Our initial vote, specifically as to the charge of murder one of Jose: six men—guilty, six women—not guilty.

The men seem to agree with us that Jose and Kitty psychologically abused their children; however, they see "no evidence whatsoever" (Roger, pounding his fist on the table for emphasis) of sexual abuse (a key element of the killing-out-of-fear scenario). They think Erik is gay and that is how he is able to describe homosexual acts. Phil thinks what Kitty "knew all along" is that Erik was gay. More than one of the men thinks that Erik and Lyle were "doing" each other!!!

Annie kept pointing out that counsel's insinuations of Erik's homosexuality in closing arguments are not evidence, and none of the women think Erik's sexuality has anything to do with whether or not he was abused or with whether or not he planned to kill his parents. I myself have joked about a Casey-Erik-Craig love triangle.

The one thing we can all agree on is that Oziel is slime! Also, that the BHPD screwed up. As Tracy says, "You can't plan luck."

My big contribution of the day was to point out that most of the evidence on both sides is circumstantial. The law says that, given two reasonable explanations for circumstantial evidence, you are supposed to choose the one that points toward innocence and ignore the one that points toward guilt. The problem here is that the men do not consider the defense to be reasonable.

The law also says that a confession alone isn't proof of a crime, and there is some question in this case as to what constitutes a confession. I'm not saying I don't think they did it—of course they did it—but I do think that all the circumstantial evidence surrounding the purchase of the guns, the "alibi," the will, postcrime spending, lying to everyone, the tapes, etc., etc., is subject to more than one reasonable interpretation (premeditation versus self-defense).

Talk radio (KABC again): Some woman astrologer was on, preparing to tell us what Lyle's and Erik's horoscopes have to say about whether or not they're going to have a good Christmas! I listened to just enough to realize she didn't even know them apart. I turned it off, this time not so much because it was the right thing to do, but because I'm sick of the Menendez brothers, and I'm sick of people who express opinions about them without even knowing which is which.

FRIDAY, DECEMBER 17, 1993

Deliberations are "The Group Project from Hell"!

We finally realized the venting we were doing was to be expected after five months of not being allowed to discuss the case even among ourselves. We started going around the table, expressing our concerns in a somewhat more civilized manner than yesterday.

The guys seem to think we were here for the defense to prove there was sexual abuse. They don't apparently understand that the "burden of proof" is on the prosecution. Frankly, without the defendants' confessions, I don't think the prosecution could have proven they even did it. I offered that I couldn't be absolutely sure that Erik was sexually abused, but that I don't have to be absolutely sure for it to raise a "reasonable doubt" in my mind as to the degree of Erik's guilt. Annie said later that she thought this was a "pivotal" point. We'll see.

Some of the men have a big problem with the fact that the expert witnesses were paid and are dismissing their testimony almost completely on that basis!

Both of the black men on our jury object strongly every time someone calls the defendants "boys," on the grounds that they are African American men who are offended by the term. I conceded that the defense's maternal treatment of the defen-

dants and calling them "boys" and dressing them in sweaters
(although it *was* freezing in the courtroom) were probably cal-
culated to elicit juror sympathy. However, a lot of the testimony was about times when "the men" were underage, and,
I'm sorry, I'm going to call even black males under the age of
eighteen "boys."

Some of us are trying to be very careful not to confuse Lyle
with Erik, but others seem to think it's perfectly legitimate to
give Erik credit/blame for things Lyle said/did/thought.

I was so exhausted today that when I stopped by the gro-
cery store on my way home from work (I keep calling it that),
I wandered the aisles in a daze, even though I had a list.

Paula, at work, has started a pool as to Erik's verdict and
the date we will reach it. I am quite amused.

MONDAY, DECEMBER 20, 1993
Today's discussions revolved around several tapes we listened to: "12/11," "JS body wire," "911," and Erik's August
21 statement to police.

Roger just *can't believe* (his emphasis) that someone as
smart as Jose who has something to hide would send his kid to
a therapist. It doesn't seem to matter if he "owned" the therapist and had Erik sign waivers of confidentiality (which, to me,
indicates a sleazy therapist who would probably rather blackmail someone than turn him in anyway) and was doing it to
avoid having the Calabasas burglaries go on Erik's record
(which, in turn, would tarnish Jose's potential political image).
[Erik, along with his brother and a couple of friends, was involved in a couple of minor burglaries, for which he took the
blame.] He just doesn't understand how hard it is for abused
kids to tell.

We all agreed that the "12/11" tape is shrouded in ulterior
motives and half-truths. I think Lyle is like a little mynah bird
with something to hide and that the whole Kitty "mercy killing" [to put her out of her misery because she was so depressed

about the way Jose treated her] is Oziel's theory and a crock. I pointed out that, if we're going to take the tape literally, greed is out, so is hatred and control. The worst thing Lyle actually said Jose was doing to Kitty, besides the affair (which was old news and unlikely to prompt a sudden desire to kill), was that he was considering going into politics and wasn't taking her to enough dinner parties! All Erik had to say was that he didn't want to hear bad things said about his father and that he regrets the killings and wishes he'd had "any other choice." Roger considers this tape, which begins and ends in the middle of a conversation, to be the most critical piece of evidence we have, although he is willing to dismiss Dr. Vicary altogether because he didn't date his notes!

Roger thinks that not only did Oziel hypnotize Judalon Smyth, but that he's satanic as well.

The guys have mentioned a couple of times how unfair it is that Jose was also on trial but wasn't here to defend himself. I gave a little speech about how if Jose *were* on trial, I don't know that I'd have enough evidence to convict him of sexual abuse. However, it seems believable enough that it raises a big, huge reasonable doubt in my mind as to the degree of *Erik's* guilt. If Jose *were* the defendant, the prosecution would have to *prove* sexual molestation. But since it's Erik on trial, all we have to do is decide if we have a reasonable doubt or not—it's up to the prosecution to *prove* there was a plan to kill. Yes, this is basically the same speech I gave last week, but it doesn't seem to be sinking in.

TUESDAY, DECEMBER 21, 1993

We all agreed on something today— that there was "intent to kill." This followed my statement that, although I could make an intellectual argument for acquittal, my true feeling is that Erik is guilty of voluntary manslaughter. I volunteered this information because we had been discussing murder one, yes or no, from the beginning, and I was afraid the men were being so obstinate because maybe they thought we all wanted acquittal or something.

Now we are debating the concept of "premeditation." We made a list of supporting and contradicting evidence, and the funny thing is that a lot of the same items are on both lists. At least we are getting down to important stuff and away from bizarre theories and speculation.

I bit the bullet today (so to speak) and looked at all the gory crime scene and autopsy photos. They were much worse up close than across the room on a bulletin board.

I suggested we have a secret vote next time so people would not be inhibited about changing their vote.

WEDNESDAY, DECEMBER 22, 1993
Today's major breakthrough was that Phil has come to his senses and admits that, although he is "more than 50 percent sure they planned it," maybe that's not enough to convict Erik of murder one.

I gave a speech on testimony that was not allowed and the various reasons why I thought that might be. I decided a long time ago that I couldn't be responsible for evidence that wasn't admitted for one reason or another, or witnesses that weren't called, or leads that weren't followed up, or questions that weren't asked.

We all learned a lesson today—I have been protesting (unsuccessfully) the wholesale request of exhibits for us to examine and testimony to be read back. It's easy enough to pass pictures around the room but kind of a hassle to check them in and out everyday if you don't really need them. I was mortified when we marched into the courtroom to hear testimony read back, only to find the judge, the attorneys, Erik, the press, and a few groupies waiting for us! I had been expecting maybe the court reporter and a couple of bailiffs. Then, because we hadn't been specific enough, we had to sit through forty-five minutes of testimony to get the five minutes that were pertinent to our discussion. For me this was pure torture. My only satisfaction was to imagine everyone speculating their little brains out as to why we wanted to hear *that*!?

I admitted that if Erik was really greedy (no evidence of it) and really stupid (*bad* plan) and really lucky (didn't get caught) and hired an attorney who was clever enough (that's possible) to make up such a complicated, consistent, believable (to me) defense and get dozens of witnesses to lie on the witness stand (unlikely), then maybe he *did* plan to kill his parents. However, I have a reasonable doubt that that's what happened, so the most I can go for is voluntary manslaughter. Even a frightened snail who goes into a room blasting a shotgun would have to expect to kill someone!

Roger reiterated that he feels the "12/11" tape is "the closest we'll ever get to knowing what really happened." I think it makes more sense in the light of placating Oziel and covering up sexual abuse than it does taken at face value. Actually, there are parts which indicate Oziel knew about the abuse, or whatever else was happening that was fear-inducing that we may never know about. For example, there is a reference to Lyle's having "rescued" Erik—rescued him from what? We have speculated endlessly as to how this forty-minute tape fits into the alleged eight-hour "therapy session."

I came up with a new theory today. We were discussing motives and wondering why Erik mentioned smelling smoke and seeing fire but did not mention ringing in his ears or sore shoulders from the kick of the shotgun. During this discussion I was looking at pictures of his incredibly messy bedroom (why didn't they just say it was a burglary?) and suddenly it came to me—aliens did it! There, in plain view, was a copy of *Communion*, by Whitley Strieber, and a sports bottle with a strange alien-looking face on it. Aliens are known to sexually violate humans, plus Erik obviously didn't need a new Rolex—there was a perfectly good Swatch lying right there on his desk!

THURSDAY, DECEMBER 23, 1993

I made a big fuss today about how we should be more careful and more specific about what testimony we have read back, and this time everyone agreed. This was *after* we heard read-back on Grant Walker and Craig Cignarelli, the latter of which no one seemed to know what we were listening for or when we'd heard enough so we could stop the court reporter.

FRIDAY, DECEMBER 24, 1993

Christmas Eve. Went to Pacific Bell in the morning to say hello and have breakfast with my co-workers.

SATURDAY, DECEMBER 25, 1993

A Christmas to remember. I spent some time yesterday with my brother Mike and his wife Jane, who are visiting from Albuquerque, at her parents' home in Torrance; that was nice, but I might have made travel plans if not for the trial. I couldn't even take Annie up on her invitation to spend Christmas with her family because we are forbidden to socialize outside of deliberations. As it was, I was sick in bed all day with a cold. At least yesterday's bad sore throat has disappeared.

MONDAY, DECEMBER 27, 1993

I heard from several friends that the newspaper carried rather detailed descriptions of the jurors today. We are starting to get paranoid about the press. They hang around like vultures waiting for us to reach a verdict or freak out or something! Part of the article was about how Tracy, Annie, and I hang out together, and how our jury is always joking around and laughing! We do things on purpose sometimes to throw them off, like joke with jurors we are not deliberating nicely with.

I got all the guys to admit, with a show of hands, that they thought Lyle and Erik had lied about the bulk of their testimony and that they [the male jurors] had *expected* they *would* lie, considering their lives are at stake. They claimed later not to have understood the question, but none of the women seemed to have been confused (none of them raised their hands; all of them thought it was *possible* they *might* lie).

TUESDAY, DECEMBER 28, 1993
   Couldn't talk today. Literally. Tried writing notes for Annie to read out loud for me, but Mike had a fit about that and we spent considerable time quietly going over our notes.

WEDNESDAY, DECEMBER 29, 1993
   I was afraid I'd be kicked off the jury [because of my laryngitis], but everyone—even George, who says it's more fun to fight with me than it would be to get rid of me—seems to want to work around me. Spent a couple of hours at Kaiser [a local HMO], only to find out what I already knew—there is no magic cure for laryngitis. I told the doctor I needed my voice back because I was on a jury that was in the middle of deliberations. He said, "*Not* the *Menendez* trial?!" When I admitted it was, he got so excited I thought he was going to pee his pants! He wanted to know if I was the juror who called in last week with the flu. I whispered, "No," but that it would probably be in the paper tomorrow that I have laryngitis and he could say he treated me!

THURSDAY, DECEMBER 30, 1993
   The bailiff was going to hook up a microphone for me this morning but instead he showed up with a little plastic red, yellow, and blue "My First Sony" tape recorder and microphone. When Annie and Tracy saw that and found out whose it was (Kuriyama's little daughter's), they laughed until they cried! It was like a baby karaoke machine, and it did the trick.
   Today there was less mention of Erik's sexuality and more references to the BBC [Billionaire Boys Club], Rolex watches,

and "Why didn't they just leave?" (see Lyle's September 21 testimony).

SATURDAY, JANUARY 1, 1994

Happy New Year! I was invited to a party last night, but I stayed home because: (1) I'm still sick and need to rest; (2) I can't talk; (3) if I could talk, I figure all people would want to talk about (to me) is the trial; and (4) I can't think of anything else to talk about *besides* the trial!

MONDAY, JANUARY 3, 1994

I can talk again! Listened to the "12/11" tape (again! arrgh!) and discussed "malice aforethought" in a semiorganized fashion. This is not an easy concept, and I have no confidence whatsoever that we all understand it. Basically, it doesn't matter to me, because if we're talking "heat of passion" (which I still think applies), "malice" automatically does not apply.

My latest theory is that Dr. Oziel and Craig Cignarelli planned these murders so they could blackmail Erik and Lyle and get rich off screenplays. Just kidding!

I am appreciating, more and more each day, the professional attitudes of the people I work with at Pacific Bell. They almost never yell in meetings or call each other names or take things personally to a degree where they can hardly think straight!

Today was the first day we really discussed the difference between the killings of Jose and Mary Louise Menendez. We had discussed possible motives for killing each of them (Jose: fear, greed, control, hatred, possible and/or actual disinheritance and/or disowning, "the [BBC] movie made me do it," etc.; Kitty: fear, mercy killing—because she was miserable/because Jose was "torturing" her/because she was already full of holes and bleeding to death, carrying out her "suicide," eliminating a witness, getting control of the estate, etc.), but so far had only actually voted yes or no on the count of murder one of Jose. Today's vote:

	Jose	Kitty
Murder one	3	5
Murder two	3	2
Voluntary MS	6	5
Involuntary MS	0	0

Talked to my friend Cindy, who found out she was pregnant around the same time I started jury duty. Her baby is due in a few weeks. She stayed home New Year's Eve for much the same reasons I did—she didn't have a dressy maternity outfit, she's physically uncomfortable, and all people can think of to talk to her about is the baby!

TUESDAY, JANUARY 4, 1994

I lost my temper today and yelled at Roger, who had interrupted me (among others) one time too many. I told him I'd get to my point if he'd just *shut up* a minute, and he responded, "You women sure are testy today." I went off on him about how I'm not "you women," I'm *Hazel*, and I'm tired of being interrupted when I've got the floor, and I'm tired of him accusing "us women" of saying and thinking things that *I* didn't say and that *I* don't necessarily think. I was all the more infuriated by Roger because we had had a conversation yesterday in which he indicated that our thinking wasn't all that far apart, in his opinion.

As to the fear element [as a motive], I keep hearing things like "I could give Erik the benefit of a doubt on Jose but not on Kitty" (because Lyle reloaded and went back in to finish her off and Erik handed him the shell, therefore "aiding and abetting" Lyle), yet none of the men are willing to use this "benefit of a doubt" to decrease their verdict from murder to manslaughter! I keep trying to get them to quantify their doubt somehow, pointing out that even I don't believe the defense 100 percent. I think there may be more to the story than we've heard, but the evidence does point to their having killed out of fear. They (Roger does most of the talking) want the *defense* to have proved *molestation* "beyond a reasonable doubt" before they'll give Erik any benefit.

Rocky thinks society would be better off if more parents raised their kids the way Jose and Kitty did!!! But then, he also evidently resents the fact that his parents never came to watch him play football and is jealous that Lyle and Erik got so much attention sports-wise. I figure there's something like that underlying each man's reluctance to be open-minded about this case. Ben has said some things about having been mistreated as a boy, and Roger says he's worked as a counselor of some kind, but I don't know why these things wouldn't make them more sympathetic instead of less. Ben is a big believer in Grant Walker's story, because his experience is that people are oblivious to the presence of repair men. Roger says things sometimes that make me think he watches Court TV or talks to someone who does. I don't know if he's just being cute or what. George is just hateful in general and thinks he knows everything because he was a police officer at one time ("There's *no way* they're going to think of picking up the shells afterward unless they planned it."). Mike is so self-righteous that "you'll *never* convince me that a twelve-year-old is going to be asking his ten-year-old cousin if it's normal for his father to be 'massaging' his dick," because when *he* was twelve years old, he *knew* it was wrong and didn't have to ask. He probably didn't have anyone trying to do it to him either. However, of the guys, Mike makes the best use of his notes to back up his arguments. Phil is the closest we have to a reasonable man in that he at least pretends to be considering other points of view and, for the most part, avoids insulting "us women." However, he does a lot of waffling and sucks at facilitating group discussions.

WEDNESDAY, JANUARY 5, 1994

Continued our last-ditch round-the-table discussion. There was a lot of stuff about what spoiled brats Erik and Lyle are, based mostly, I guess, on how much money they spent after the killings. Never mind that their father was a millionaire and the whole family had been spending more than the rest of us all their lives. I think these guys are just jealous. Annie exploded when Roger mentioned Erik's "extracurricular activities," thinking he meant his homosexuality again (which Roger denies having meant this time, but which he has said many times before) and gave another lecture on how we shouldn't be discussing things that aren't evidence.

THURSDAY, JANUARY 6, 1994

These guys (I hate to lump them all together after my tirade on Tuesday, but they're all driving me crazy) can't even let us get to our point without jumping in and interrupting for one reason or another. I don't know why they take everything so personally. Today Tracy was calmly trying to point out the irony in their willingness to believe Erik is homosexual based on pure speculation versus their unwillingness to believe the evidence that he was molested. This point was lost entirely on the men, and the discussion degenerated into another big fight.

I personally think speculation is fine, even necessary—I think of it as a type of brainstorming for ideas—but I think it would be unfair to convict someone of first-degree murder based on speculation. One of the problems is that not all evidence is believable to all jurors, but some of them don't seem to be able to distinguish between "evidence" and "proof." Sometimes when they say there's "no evidence whatsoever" I think they *must* mean no hard, or *direct*, evidence, or no evidence that they *believe*, or not *enough* evidence, which is fine, but it always leads to an argument. Almost all the evidence in this whole case on both sides is circumstantial.

Phil's big thing is that, although he thinks Erik's sexuality may have caused some of the tension in the family, he wants us to be sure to understand he's not homophobic. Well, maybe not, but even if that's true, I don't think he can speak for the other men.

Here is a teeny, tiny example of the millions of little details that we have been arguing about for three weeks now (I think there are still teeth marks in my purse strap from biting it to keep from screaming): We had testimony read back which says that [a couple of days before the killings] Lyle, from inside the guest house, heard Erik and Kitty screaming outside the guest house, Kitty having chased Erik there from the main house. On X-exam he said he heard them screaming "from the main house," which, to me, could mean from clear *inside* the main house or simply from the *direction* of the main house as they were running outside toward the guest house. After all that, back in the jury room, Rocky (or was it Mike?) misquoted him, saying, "See, I *told* you Lyle said he heard them 'from somewhere inside the main house.' " All this has something to do with whether or not the maid would/should/could have heard the argument if, in fact, it occurred.

On the brighter side, we discovered there were two people (Ben and George) who thought all along that the boys burst into the family room from two different doors, which could possibly indicate a higher level of planning than if it had been only one door. Others didn't even remember there being another door, so we looked at the floor plan and heard testimony read back which settled it (there are two doors, not counting the outside French doors, but they only burst through one of them, like I thought), but it didn't change anyone's vote.

Phil thinks that you could go into any family photo album and take isolated events and construct a child abuse case against the parents. I think he's probably right, but, as Annie pointed out, in most families there would be people who would come forward and say, "It didn't happen."

Speaking of families, if my brother was killed by his children, and I thought the reason was because they were evil, greedy brats, I doubt seriously that I would testify on their behalf!

Based on a minor incident with the press yesterday, we are now being escorted to a special (dismal, boring) area for breaks and guarded like prisoners. Even so, it is always nice to see the alternates' friendly faces and to talk about something else for a change. The judge was going to have us escorted to lunch as a group (everyone I have ever heard of has done this during deliberations, but then, their lunch is usually paid for too—not us!), but we begged and whined until he agreed not to.

FRIDAY, JANUARY 7, 1994

Now we've done it—the whole world now knows what an issue Erik's sexuality has become in our deliberations because we requested a reread of testimony that pertains specifically to that subject. It was Annie's idea—she wasn't expecting it would change anyone's mind, but she wanted to send a message to the judge that this was an issue. Erik was mortified; you could tell by looking at him. The only relevant testimony was Erik's own—that Kitty accused him of not being man enough to keep a girlfriend (after being with her a year!), that Jose called him a "faggot," and that Erik was afraid to talk about the molestation for fear people would think he was gay. George's comment, immediately upon our return to the jury room, was, "See, I *told* you we could talk about 'faggots.'"

I didn't realize it until today, but I guess I'm Queen of the Jury. Rocky and I had a one-on-one debate this morning about something or other he said I said yesterday, which wasn't accurate anyway (I think he even lost sleep over it). He concluded, "You aren't the only one in here; there are twelve of us and you only have one vote." I couldn't have been more surprised! I asked him why, since I'm only one of twelve people, it matters so much to him what I say, and, if it matters so much, why doesn't he *listen* to what I'm saying instead of just assuming what I mean? He indicated that he thinks I have a lot of influence, or something like that (God forbid I should try to quote anyone at this point!), which is ridiculous—we are six very strong women with our own, albeit fairly compatible, viewpoints, and I may have upset a few of the men, but I have no evidence that I've influenced any of them!

We are, however, entering the compromise phase of deliberations. Phil, Mike, Roger, and Marta all made nice little speeches about how they were willing to stretch their minds and their votes, perhaps to Jose-voluntary manslaughter and Kitty-murder two, for the sake of reaching a verdict. I am not, however, inclined to change my vote at this point (voluntary manslaughter for both), and I think Rocky, George, and Ben are all still stuck on murder one for both.

I keep hoping that someone will be able to come up with something that will solve this case once and for all—either way, I don't care. We all say we don't want to see an innocent man punished or a guilty man set free, including me.

The only new things we came up with today support, in my opinion, fear [as a motive]: If Lyle put extra shells in his pocket, why didn't he use them? Did he forget about them in his panic? If he's lying, and did reload from his pockets before going to the car to get that last shell for Kitty, why did the neighbors only hear around eight shots (the number of shells physically accounted for)? Why lie about having put them in your pocket if you're going to volunteer that you went after one last shell? Why say you went after one last shell if there were no witnesses and you could get away with it, unless your goal was to tell the complete truth? What kind of a plan would involve running out to a car in front of the house where you could be seen with your guns? Why lie about the location of the car if you're going to volunteer that you went after one last shell? (I haven't explored nearly all the pertinent issues in this journal, but as you can see, the questions are endless.)

Also, according to Lyle, his parents were rising from the

couch; according to Erik they were standing; the wounds and bloodstains also indicate they were standing at some point— did they hear them coming and get up to see what the noise was? Were Erik and Lyle in such a panic/hurry that they approached noisily on the hard foyer floor, as opposed to sneaking up on them quietly?

Also, back to the gay thing, if Erik was confused about why it was so important to Kitty that he get a girlfriend and only later, after they broke up, did Kitty accuse him of not being man enough to keep her, wouldn't that indicate that he wasn't gay? Sure, he questioned it himself because of what he says his father was doing to him, but if he knew he was gay, he wouldn't wonder what Kitty's problem was—he would already know, wouldn't he?

Because there seemed to be some confusion, I asked if anyone thinks a man who is having sex with his underage son is necessarily gay. Everyone said no—he's a child molester. I asked if a boy who is having sex with his father is gay—no, he's an abused child. OK, next question—does the fact that a man openly ridicules gays mean he cannot be having sex with his son? Basically, Rocky does have a hard time with this one (if anyone else thought it too, they let Rocky take the heat). He also thinks that, magically, on his eighteenth birthday, Erik became a man and, therefore, a homosexual because he let his father keep doing it to him. Yesterday George's position (among others') was, evidently, that Jose's calling Erik a faggot makes him a faggot!!! This is what we're dealing with!

An ironic thing happened at break this morning: we saw the entire cast of "Beverly Hills 90210," Kitty Menendez's coveted zip code! They were going out the back way, having just finished filming a courtroom wedding scene. I could probably have lived without the experience, but we wouldn't have seen them if they hadn't started guarding us like prisoners during break. Shannen Doherty looked awful.

SUNDAY, JANUARY 9, 1994

Well, it's been three weeks, and I see no hope whatsoever
of our reaching a verdict. I *really* hate that it's turned into a
men-versus-women thing. However, contrary to stereotype, if
you ask me, it's the men who tend to get emotional about what
they're saying (they practically leap across the table at you, and
they can't understand "heat of passion"?!), and they try des-
perately to defend their positions but are hard-pressed to back
them up with evidence. The women appear to me to be much
more open-minded, much more respectful of other people's
opinions, and, while we sometimes get excited and frustrated
too, we never resort to insults and name-calling like they do
(not to their faces, anyway). I wonder if public consensus is
also divided along gender lines? I hate to think that this group
of six men is representative of all men. The ironic thing is that
both Roger and Ben have told me they think I'm a pretty logical thinker. I wonder if they were just sucking up to me?

I am very proud of the women in this group. We all agree,
more or less, but not on every detail. Each one of us has different insights and good points to make. Some are better than
others at biting their tongues and speaking up when appropriate, and some are visibly growing in those areas.

The way we left it Friday was that we had discussed everything we could think of, there were no outstanding testimony
or evidence requests, and I have no idea what will happen tomorrow. We toyed all week with the idea of telling the judge
we give up, and at this point I feel that I have done everything
I can and that giving up would be OK with me. It has been
quite a challenge to try to remain objective and open to new
insights while offering my opinions and trying to convince others of what I feel is the right thing to do.

MONDAY, JANUARY 10, 1994

Mike began the week by taking back his offer to compromise, saying he couldn't live with himself if he voted less than
murder one on both counts. Those of us who weren't inclined

to change our votes either supported his decision completely. It's not like he's the only holdout! We discussed what would happen if we didn't reach a verdict, and, since none of us knows, and since we aren't supposed to consider penalty when determining guilt, and since there seems to be no hope for a consensus, we went ahead and did it—we told the judge we were deadlocked. We sat around the jury room most of the day until he called us into the courtroom, talked to us for two minutes, and sent us back in. We may have him elaborate on a couple of points of law before we give up for good. Today's vote:

	Jose	Kitty
Murder one	5	5
Murder two	1	3
Voluntary MS	6	4
Involuntary MS	0	0

The media was all hot-to-trot when we left. They still aren't at liberty to talk to us, but there were five times as many cameras and people outside as usual.

TUESDAY, JANUARY 11, 1994

Now my *other* worst nightmare has come true: on the radio Joe Crummey (KFI) was talking about how stupid we are because we can't agree on the obvious—that Erik is guilty of murder. He not only compared us to the Denny jury, he suggested that we probably *are* the Denny jury and that they just moved us from one case to the other!

WEDNESDAY, JANUARY 12, 1994

We requested further clarification from the judge regarding "malice." We knew one of the differences between first- and second-degree murder was premeditation, but we only just realized that first-degree murder requires "express" malice, as opposed to "implied" malice. So then we had to agree on what "express" means. None of these things legally means what you always thought they meant.

Anyway, as we walked through the courtroom for a break, Abramson was sitting there with her arms folded, looking pissed off. My guess is that she thought we were trying to decide between first- and second-degree murder, based on our request, so I smiled at her. Both Annie and Tracy, who came after me, reported that she flashed smiles at them, so maybe I reassured her a little.

Marta took the men on single-handedly regarding the issue of money (she is the only one of us who has any). She called them bigots and resorted to foul language, which worked about as well as you'd expect, but I guess it was worth a try! A direct quote: "How much do you think this fucking Christian Dior suit cost me?" Her best point was that the spending they did was in keeping with their former life style.

Sandi called to rag on me for not reaching a verdict today so she could win the pool at work. I told her I thought whoever came the closest without going over, which would be her, should win.

A Little Homicide Review:

First-degree murder = intent to kill + express malice + premeditation

Second-degree murder = intent to kill + express or implied malice (not enough evidence to prove premeditation)

Sudden quarrel/heat-of-passion killing qualifies as manslaughter (applies to honest but *un*reasonable belief of imminent danger)

Voluntary manslaughter = intent to kill

Involuntary manslaughter = no intent to kill

Acquittal = pure self-defense = not a crime (reasonable belief in necessity to protect one's self)

THURSDAY, JANUARY 13, 1994

We have made no progress since Monday, so we told the judge again that we are deadlocked. He gave us new verdict forms and new instructions that, for the life of me, sounded just like Monopoly rules. Do not pass GO; do not collect $200.

Roger stunned us all this morning by saying he thought there had been a problem from day one with burden of proof (I agree!). He then proceeded to say, "It's not up to the prosecution to prove murder one . . . well, it's not up to them to prove that the killings were, well . . . never mind." Later he was adamant about taking a final vote after everyone else already thought we'd taken our final vote. He said he hadn't understood it that way, and, when I wondered aloud what else he hadn't understood all along, we got into it again. He pouted, refused to change his vote, then changed it after all because we wouldn't let him vote twice on conspiracy (he had given Jose and Kitty different verdicts). Ben (among others) backed him up on voting twice! I just can't *believe* the you're-not-the-boss-of-me attitude of some of these grown men. The whole thing degenerated into another big fight. I wasn't personally upset by any of this, but Annie and Roger, and Linda and George (who was calling us "ignorant asses" again), got into it good. Even Phil was embarrassed by the other men and threatened to walk out if they kept it up.

OK, so we were called into the courtroom one last time—it was standing room only—and the judge thanked us for our service and declared it a mistrial. It was all really kind of sad. The press doesn't know the final vote, and we are not to speak to them until the other jury comes out with a verdict.

Post-Trial

After that we got our chance to speak to the attorneys if we wanted, which was weird, because I had to walk right past the prosecution team if I wanted to speak to the defense team. It was also kind of eerie talking to people I feel I know well but have never before spoken to. Marcia Morrissey is cool (she's kind of fidgety during examination, though, and needs to stand up straight). She said I was their favorite juror (I think because they could always read my facial expressions so easily), and I responded, "I'll bet you say that to all the girls!" Leslie Abramson took my hand, hugged me, and said, "Hazel, I love you!" I dubbed her a legal goddess in return. We exchanged notes and gossip on deliberations and on the other jurors and agreed to discuss it further at a later date. They wanted to know what they should do differently next time, and I said, "Pick a better jury!" I found out some amazing things about my fellow (male) jurors that I hesitate to put in writing, and was told that the other prospective jurors were even worse (she [Abramson] calls them "Death Row") but that they were running out of challenges.

I did not speak to Lester Kuriyama (Tracy critiqued his performance at length to his face—none of that "barking ferret" nonsense next time!) except to shake his hand and thank him for the baby karaoke machine. He made it a special point to tell me that they think I am very smart and that his wife's name is Hazel. I think that's what he said, it was kind of a blur. I wonder who "they" are and how "they" concluded that I'm smart without ever having spoken to me, and why he felt he needed to tell me that?

After we turned in our badges and everything, we got a police escort through the secret back way, in a bus outfitted to transport prisoners, to the parking garage. Despite all that, we were accosted inside the garage by many camera people from unknown origin(s) and a woman handing out "Front Page" [a tabloid TV show] business cards. I wrote on mine, "Accosted us in garage," so I could keep track.

Went out for a drink with Annie, Tracy, and Betty at the Irish bar, and we told our true theories about what happened and agreed to stay friends. When I got home I had several phone messages (including one from my mom, who heard the news in Idaho before I even left the courthouse) and a letter from "Inside Edition," which had obviously been hand-delivered to my mailbox that evening. [So much for anonymity.]

FRIDAY, JANUARY 14, 1994

Let's see, since last night I've heard from Mom, Don, Michael and Jane, Jerry, Sandi, Sonja, Kendell and Monique, Lonna and Martin, and Tim. I haven't heard from the media, but then, we *are* under orders not to talk yet, and my phone *is* unlisted. [Being a Pacific Bell employee, I was easy for them to track down upon my return to work.] I took today off work—I'm not ready to face all those people yet.

Leslie Abramson called to invite me (and all the women jurors) to dinner, and we talked for at least an hour. She had the same idea I did—that we might want to find a reputable news program and appear as a group to tell our story (she calls it "taking her girls on the road"). She said, among many other things, that Ben has already made a deal with "Hard Copy." That sounds so sleazy. If I agree to do any publicity at all, I will have to be confident of our ability to portray ourselves credibly and not come off as a bunch of whiny, vindictive, bleeding-heart women.

Abramson said it was the judge's choice not to allow the attorneys to question the potential jurors and that he reversed his original decision at the last minute—it's the result of a proposition that was voted in a couple of years ago, and since then there have been many more hung juries than usual.

I remembered to ask her my question this time: what did she think the defense was going to be before she found out about the sexual abuse? She says she didn't know for sure and she thought she was going to lose big-time (they were going to pay her either way).

She says I was Erik's "rock," meaning it meant a lot to him when I smiled and let him know I was still on his side (which only happened inadvertently, because most of the time I couldn't see his face from where I was sitting, and when I wasn't busy weighing evidence, I was busy trying to hide my feelings from the press). I don't know if she's putting me on or not—I'm naturally suspicious, as if I were still a juror—but even if it turns out he has another "rock" or two in the bunch, I think she's sincere in her appreciation.

SATURDAY, JANURARY 15, 1994
Watched my videotape of the closing arguments, not because I want to relive them so soon, but because I was curious about the accompanying commentary. I was pleasantly surprised to hear that Terry Moran [of Court TV], although ex-

tremely professional and objective, I thought, leaned slightly toward the defense and had some complimentary things to say about Abramson. I have therefore elevated him out of the "vulture" category.

Here is my courtroom/bird-watching analogy:

judge = wise old owl	press = vultures
jury = penguins	groupies = sea gulls
attorneys = peacocks	witnesses = canaries
defendants = sitting ducks	Det. Zoeller = ostrich

SUNDAY, JANUARY 16, 1994

I'm waiting for the other shoe to drop. I asked Abramson, "So now, what are we going to hear about Erik that we didn't know and will piss us off?" She said that we had already heard about the Calabasas burglaries and that there's nothing else. I know a lot of people hate her—I think I can handle that. I know a lot of people are going to hate the fact that we were a hung jury, both from a waste-of-taxpayer-money standpoint and a how-could-you-not-convict-him-of-murder standpoint.

There are some things about Judge Stanley Weisberg that bother me: I don't know how unfair it was of him not to let the attorneys question the potential jurors, or not to allow "perfect self-defense" (none of us wanted it anyway), but I do think he was biased against the defense for whatever reason, and I was amazed that he didn't keep our deadlock out of the press until the other jury had reached a verdict.

I keep wondering if there's anything I could have done to prevent a hung jury: be more persuasive? change my vote? report fellow jurors for things I couldn't prove (bias, exposure to outside information, stupidity)? I don't think so. Tracy wrote a note to the judge early in deliberations about some of us evidently not understanding "evidence" and "burden of proof." She was humiliated and we were all discouraged from asking further questions when her note came back marked,

"See pages such-and-such of instructions," and was passed around the room for all to see. Like we hadn't thought of that. Later, Annie got brave and wrote a note describing the kinds of things we were hearing in the jury room that indicated a pretrial bias and/or exposure to outside information. She didn't know if it would matter to the judge, and she did not get a response, but she felt better (and so did I). Even when our foreman wrote official group notes we didn't get much help from the judge.

I am also wondering when would be an appropriate time to end this journal? Lyle's jury is still deliberating. Who knows what the future holds for Lyle, Erik, their attorneys, their juries, the justice system, the fields of psychology and child abuse, etc., as a result of this trial?

[One thing that the future held for us was the 6.8 earthquake in Northridge, which occurred on January 17, 1994, the day after my last diary entry.]

COMMENTARIES

Psychological Commentary on the Diary

Lawrence S. Wrightsman and Amy J. Posey

The publication of a juror's diary is a noteworthy event for a number of reasons. First, only a few exist. When General William Westmoreland sued CBS Television for libel in 1984, one of the jurors did dutifully keep a daily record of court happenings (Roth, 1986), but this trial was terminated in midstream, with no opportunity for the jury to deliberate. One of the jurors in the trial of Bernhard Goetz, the "subway vigilante," prepared a daily memoir of the trial's developments that was especially helpful in showing how the jury logically reached what was, for many observers, an unpopular verdict (Lesly, 1988). A long article in the *New Yorker* magazine by one of its staff writers about his experiences as a juror and his reactions to them is another of the very few published, extended accounts of a person's jury service (Finnegan, 1994).

Lawyers and to some extent judges speculate about the impact on jurors of the various events of a trial, including the testimony and actions of the witnesses and the behavior of the attorneys. Occasionally, trial attorneys or journalists capitalize on the opportunity to quiz jurors after a trial about what had the greatest effect on them (see Brill, 1984; Villaseñor, 1977). But the impact of such "as-told-to" accounts pales compared to the opportunity to see the trial unfold from Hazel Thornton's daily vantage point of the jury box.

This diary is also important because in the last twenty years, psychology, communication studies, and other social sciences have focused on the trial jury as a means of testing some of their central theories. The trial jury has accordingly generated extensive and intensive research and a number of provocative findings from which a science of jury behavior is beginning to emerge. Some conclusions are firm; others depend more on the nature of the particular case and jury.

But most of this social science knowledge is based on studies that use *simulations* of juries that manipulate some identifiable factor (such as whether the defendant takes the stand) in an effort to determine whether that factor is influential across cases, juries, and settings. So a diary such as Thornton's provides a rare chance to use empirical data to assess some of the conclusions of two decades of research.

Our goal is not to critique the merits of this juror's reactions or the jury's verdict. We believe that Thornton's diary reflects an intellect actively trying to make sense of the conflicting testimony and the impenetrable instructions that were presented. Conscientious people who are motivated to do a good job—which we believe the vast majority of jurors to be—can still disagree as to the proper interpretation of the evidence and of the judge's instructions about the law. We believe that this is what happened in the Erik Menendez trial, as Thornton's diary documents.

We should note, however, our distress over the general public's reaction to the outcome of the first trials of Lyle and Erik Menendez, as people complained that the brothers "got off" because the juries sympathized with them. No evidence for such sympathy emerges from this diary. In fact, *every* juror voted to convict Erik; the division that led to the hung jury was over whether he should be convicted of first-degree murder or for voluntary manslaughter. Even the lesser of these crimes carries a long prison sentence in California.

Assumptions Made by the Legal System

While it is regrettable that neither the Lyle nor the Erik Menendez jury could agree on which charge to convict, the difference of opinion among jurors reflects a fundamental assumption of psychology: people evaluate evidence differently. The word "assumption" is the key here, because our commentary is organized around the legal system's long-held assumptions about the nature of jurors and juries. We propose that the psychological research findings—and the contents of this juror's diary—challenge many of these assumptions.

Assumption 1: Jurors Are Unbiased

The American legal system provides all criminal defendants with the right to have their case heard by a jury of their peers, thus assigning to the ordinary citizen a very important role in dispensing justice. In conferring such responsibility on the jury, the founders of our legal system made several assumptions about the characteristics of the individual jurors and the jury as a whole. One such assumption is that the jury is an unbiased body capable of leaving all previously held thoughts, feelings, and ideas that might be relevant to the case at the courthouse door in order to make a decision based solely on the facts presented in the trial. Acknowledging that not everyone will be able to meet this standard, the system includes a jury selection process designed to eliminate hopelessly biased jurors.

Assumption 2: Jurors Focus Only on the Evidence During the Trial

The second assumption is that jurors are capable of reaching a decision based only on the testimony of witnesses and the physical evidence, disregarding all nonevidentiary information. They may not allow themselves to be influenced by such nonevidence as attorneys' opening statements and closing arguments, any comment made in the courtroom that is stricken from the record, the physical appearance of the defendant and other trial participants, and anything written or said about the case in the media. Whether jurors can actually meet this standard is difficult to determine; often even the jurors themselves are not able to say whether they were persuaded by an inflammatory but inadmissible statement by an attorney or a gasp from courtroom spectators.

Assumption 3: Jurors Remember and Comprehend the Evidence and Instructions

Third, along with focusing only on the evidence, jurors are assumed to be able to process and understand this evidence accurately. Many times they must listen to weeks of testimony without taking any notes. Can the average person organize and recall so much information presented over such a long span of time? Jurors are also often confronted with conflicting expert testimony and expected to determine its relative accuracy. In our increasingly complex and specialized society, is this a realistic expectation of a jury of ordinary citizens? In addition, jurors frequently hear conflicting testimony from witnesses. How is the average person expected to discern who is telling the truth and who is lying? Finally, jurors are often given complicated legal instructions that they are to follow to reach a fair and informed verdict.

Assumption 4: Jurors Can Suspend Judgment

Our legal system's fourth assumption about jurors is that they can suspend judgment until all evidence has been presented. In reality, however, what is the likelihood that a juror will be able to listen to testimony and attorneys' arguments for several hours, let alone several weeks or months, and avoid reaching some conclusion?

Assumption 5: Jurors Deliberate Only on the Evidence

Finally, the American legal system assumes that during deliberations a jury discusses only the evidence presented in the trial and that every member of the jury will have an equal opportunity to be heard. But in fact, in addition to considering the evidence, juries are likely to share relevant personal experiences and opinions about the personalities and behaviors of trial participants. To what extent do these pieces of nonevidence influence the verdict? If one member of a jury disagrees with the rest, what is the chance that that individual will speak up, and how will the rest of the jury respond to the dissenter? How does a jury deal with the prospect of being deadlocked, unable to reach a verdict? Because jury deliberations go on behind closed doors, we generally have no way of answering these questions.

Does the empirical evidence support these assumptions? In the following sections of this commentary, we shall examine what Thornton's diary reveals about the legitimacy of each of these assumptions as well as potential applicability of psychological research conclusions based on empirical studies.

ASSUMPTION 1: JURORS ARE UNBIASED

As stated, our legal system assumes that people are capable of leaving any previously held attitudes that might be relevant to the case behind upon assuming the role of juror. However, psychologists know that this is not always possible, for people bring to any new experience all past experiences and the attitudes they have formed based on those experiences. Knowing this, what conclusions can we draw based on the attitudes and experiences of specific jurors?

Demographics

Research on the effects of such basic characteristics as gender, race, age, level of education, and occupation on trial outcome suggests that there is not a simple correlation among variables. For example, Hastie, Penrod, and Pennington (1983) examined the verdicts of sixty-nine mock juries in Massachusetts and found that no single demographic characteristic correlated with the verdict in a murder trial. However, this does not mean that demographics are *never* important in determining verdicts; rather, the relationship is complicated and often depends on the specific facts of the case. In the trial of Erik Menendez, gender was clearly an important determinant of the extent to which jurors agreed or disagreed with defense arguments, as all female jurors voted for manslaughter and all males voted for murder. It is possible that something about the socialization and experiences of the women led them to be more likely to accept the argument that the Menendez brothers believed that their parents were plotting to kill them on the night of the murders. In another murder case with different circumstances, this gender split is not likely to have been present. (See Foreword for additional gender-split discussion.)

Personality

If demographics do not allow for clear-cut predictions of verdicts, what do personality characteristics reveal? Our underlying beliefs and ways of responding to the world may indeed tell us more about verdict preference than more superficial demographic variables. One often-studied personality characteristic is Rotter's (1966) concept of the locus of control. Those believing that their fate is determined primarily by their own actions are said to possess an internal locus of control, while those that believe that their fate is determined chiefly by forces outside of and not controlled by the self have an external locus of control. Research has demonstrated that, when the evidence is ambiguous, people tend to project their own locus of control onto others. Thus, people with an internal locus of control will believe that not only they but others are responsible for their own behavior. In mock jury research, this tendency leads jurors with an internal locus to perceive defendants as being more responsible for their behavior and therefore to assign harsher punishments than those with an external locus (Phares & Wilson, 1972). However, when presented with a great deal of evidence, as in an actual trial, the relationship between locus of control and verdict disappears (Kassin & Wrightsman, 1988).

A second personality characteristic that is often studied in relation to jury decision-making is Lerner's (1970) concept of belief in a just world, or the notion that people get what they deserve. Jury decisions by people with a strong belief in a just world generally go in one of two directions. In many cases, these jurors are harsher on defendants, because "bad people deserve to be punished" (Gerbasi, Zuckerman, & Reis, 1977). However, in rape cases these same jurors are relatively lenient on defendants, because they perceive rape victims as somewhat deserving of their fate (Rubin & Peplau, 1975). As with locus of control, belief in a just world does not appear to be a strong predictor of jury verdicts in actual cases (Kassin & Wrightsman, 1988).

This ambiguous relationship between verdicts and personality characteristics does not exist for the authoritarian personality, which is defined by Adorno and his colleagues (1950) as rigid, ethnocentric, sexually inhibited, politically conservative, intolerant of dissent, and highly punitive. Overall, research shows that people high in authoritarianism tend to be more likely to impose punitive sentences than those low in authoritarianism (Narby, Cutler, & Moran, 1993). However, the very nature of this personality type leads to some exceptions. While authoritarians will generally be more likely to convict in general, they are less likely to convict when the defendant is in a position of power (e.g., a police officer) or when the crime was committed to uphold authoritarian values (e.g., assaulting someone because he is gay) (Garcia & Griffitt, 1978; Hamilton, 1976).

It is possible that some of the men on the Erik Menendez jury were at least somewhat authoritarian, as they are described as believing that Erik is a homosexual, despite a lack of evidence. Some felt that he had never been sexually abused by his father but was able to describe sex acts based on his experiences with other boys. Others felt that even if he had had sex with his father, the fact that he continued to do so after he turned eighteen was proof that he was not an abused but a willing participant. Both types of jurors believed that because Erik was a homosexual and a liar, he should be convicted of murder and punished accordingly (see the diary entries for December 16 and January 7).

Voir Dire

Because the American legal system acknowledges that some jurors will arrive with biases (such as an authoritarian personality) that are virtually impossible to leave behind, it allows for a somewhat elaborate process of jury selection, known as voir dire, during which either the judge or the attorneys question prospective jurors in an attempt to reveal prejudicial opinions. What is the likelihood that a juror will honestly admit to being biased during this process? Are jurors more likely to be honest when questioned by an authority figure, such as the judge, or by the attorneys? A study found that jurors were more candid when responding to questions by attorneys during voir dire. Results further showed that when attorneys utilized a more personal, relaxed style of questioning, juror responses were more honest than when they used a formal style similar to that of judges (Jones, 1987). Could it be that jurors become nervous about being negatively evaluated by a judge and therefore lie about their biases? Marshall and Smith (1986) surveyed former jurors about their honesty during voir dire. Those who reported feeling nervous, hesitant, self-conscious, and anxious during the process were less likely to be honest than those who were relaxed. If being questioned by the judge leads prospective jurors to become overly nervous about their responses, it appears that, at least in terms of uncovering pretrial bias, attorney-conducted voir dire is more effective.

In the Menendez trial, prospective jurors filled out extensive questionnaires regarding their backgrounds and attitudes on a variety of sensitive issues such as child abuse (July 1); the attorneys, certainly, had access to these questionnaires. However, voir dire, which focused primarily on the death penalty, was conducted by the judge. Thornton remarks that a lot of people seemed to be changing their answers at this point and may have been nervous or lying (July 14). Prospective jurors might have been more relaxed and honest had the questioning been done by the attorneys. However, this is balanced somewhat against the fact that prospective jurors were questioned privately about personal items, thus eliminating the influence of other jurors' responses and the court's reactions to those responses (July 15).

Pretrial Publicity

In high-profile cases, such as the Menendez trial, jurors often have been exposed to pretrial media coverage for months or years before they are even summoned for jury duty. This creates a situation in which jurors have a factual basis for pretrial bias. What opinions have they formed as a result of this pretrial publicity? Without attorney-directed voir dire, it may be difficult to determine.

As Thornton describes, there was a separate publicity questionnaire and subsequent individually sequestered voir dire (June 28, July 1). Again, however, the questioning was conducted by the judge, and it is possible that some jurors' pretrial bias went undetected as a result (December 27, January 16).

Death Qualification

Thornton describes the questions asked of prospective jurors regarding their attitudes toward capital punishment, including, "If you found someone guilty . . . and the trial entered the penalty phase, would you always vote for death? always vote for life?" (July 14). If a potential juror answers in the affirmative to either question, he or she is removed from the jury. What remains is a "death-qualified" jury, one that is willing to sentence the defendant to death under some circumstances. Is this still a representative jury? Research suggests that eliminating people who would never impose the death penalty amounts to eliminating a significant number of women, blacks, the poor, and members of certain religious groups. People who do qualify for death-qualified juries tend to be more concerned with the crime rate, hold more favorable attitudes toward law enforcement officials, and are intolerant of procedures designed to protect the accused. Perhaps most importantly, such juries are more likely to convict than those that include people opposed to the death penalty (Fitzgerald & Ellsworth, 1984; Thompson, Cowan, Ellsworth, & Harrington, 1984; Vidmar & Ellsworth, 1974).

What kind of effects did death qualification have on the verdicts in the Menendez trial? Based on the finding that death-qualified juries tend to be more punitive, it is possible that had the Erik Menendez jury included people opposed to the death penalty it would have yielded more votes in favor of manslaughter rather than murder. All that we can do is speculate at this point.

In sum, although the legal system acknowledges that some prospective jurors may be biased, it is not always possible to recognize those biases and eliminate those jurors. Jurors may not be willing to reveal their biases, or they simply may not recognize that they have any biases. In addition, the individual characteristics that are obvious to the court (e.g., race, gender, age, etc.) are often not predictive of verdicts. As a result, it is very difficult, if not impossible, to empanel a jury of twelve "blank slates," capable of hearing the evidence free of the influence of past experiences and attitudes.

ASSUMPTION 2: JURORS FOCUS ONLY ON THE EVIDENCE DURING THE TRIAL

Once a jury has been chosen, its members are given the responsibility of listening carefully to the evidence and then rendering a decision based on the strength of the evidence alone. This requires that jurors do not allow any nonevidentiary information to influence their decision.

Opening Statements

Two such pieces of nonevidence, and the only ones that are inherently a part of the trial procedure, are the opening statements and closing arguments made by the attorneys. Opening statements generally serve as a preview of the evidence to be presented in the trial and help jurors to organize and recall that evidence by providing an information-processing framework. However, research in cognitive psychology has demonstrated that we often use our preexisting cognitive frameworks to fill in the gaps in a story with information that we never actually received. For example, when people read a story about someone who visits the doctor, they often later "recall" events in the story that did not actually take place (e.g., a nurse taking the patient's blood pressure), because such events fit the cognitive framework for what happens at the doctor's office (Bower, Black, & Turner, 1979).

What is the likelihood that jurors will fill in gaps in the evidence to match the stories provided them by an attorney's opening statement? Pyszczynski and his colleagues (1981) examined the effects of opening statements in mock trials. They found that a strong opening statement is very persuasive, even when the evidence does not support all of the claims that were made by the attorney. Unless the opposing attorney pointed out an unsupported alibi claim, mock jurors who heard that the defendant had an alibi were more likely to vote for acquittal than those who heard no such claim.

What kind of influence did the opening statements have on jurors in the Menendez case? Thornton states that the opening statements were "riveting" and that she was "glued to the edge of my seat" while listening to them (July 20). She goes on to point out that the statement made by prosecuting attorney Lester Kuriyama was not all that surprising, brief, and to the point. However, Thornton describes the defense's opening statement in more detail, especially the cognitive framework provided for them by defense attorney Leslie Abramson. In telling jurors, in some detail, of the "years of mental, emotional, physical, and sexual abuse supposedly suffered by the boys . . . for so many years," Abramson gave the jurors a story through which to interpret the evidence as well as a possible explanation for the killings.

Closing Arguments

After all the evidence has been presented, attorneys are given an additional opportunity to provide jurors with another piece of nonevidence in their closing arguments. Although jurors are generally informed by the judge that the closing arguments are not evidence, attorneys have very few restrictions as to what they may say to the jury before it is sent off to deliberate. Often this leads to dramatic attempts to appeal to the emotions of the jury in a competition to make the strongest last impression. For example, Thornton notes that the prosecutor, Kuriyama, stood directly in front of a bulletin board bearing gruesome pictures of the murder scene while making his closing arguments, and that Abramson stuck pins in a photograph of Erik's genitals in an effort to demonstrate what he claims his father did to him as a child (December 13).

Although such emotional demonstrations are quite common, closing arguments are supposed to be limited to the evidence and to logical inferences from the evidence. Inflammatory statements and appeals to the jurors' prejudices are discouraged. While the prosecution team merely hinted at their theory that Erik is homosexual during the trial (November 19), they referred to it directly in their closing arguments (December 15). As the bulk of Thornton's description of the deliberations indicates, this bit of nonevidence was perhaps the predominant topic of debate between the men and the women on his jury.

Inadmissible Evidence

An additional source of nonevidence, and one that is not an inherent part of the trial procedure, is the presentation of information, usually in the form of verbal remarks, that is ruled by the court to be inadmissible. When the judge admonishes the jury to "disregard that last statement," what is the likelihood that they will be able (or willing) to do so? Most empirical evidence suggests that jurors are not only generally incapable of disregarding inadmissible statements, but that they are even more influenced by them after being admonished by the judge (Sue, Smith, & Caldwell, 1973; Wolf & Montgomery, 1977).

These findings are consistent with the concept of psychological reactance, whereby a threat to an individual's freedom to choose to perform a certain behavior leads to a greater likelihood that the person will engage in that behavior than if no threat were present (Brehm, 1966). Thus when a judge instructs jurors that they must disregard inadmissible testimony, it is quite possible that the jury will consequently pay *more* attention to that piece of testimony than if they had received no admonition. It should come as no surprise, then, that when a statement made by Erik's friend Craig Cignarelli about the two of them dreaming of a "Billionaire Boys Club" was ordered stricken from the record, Thornton comments that it was not likely that the jury would actually forget such a remark (July 26). Indeed, the subject did come up again, at least briefly, during deliberations (December 30).

Physical Appearance

Jurors are constantly exposed to a great deal of nonevidentiary information in addition to that presented by the attorneys or the witnesses. For example, they may look to the reaction of a defendant while someone is testifying against him, or be influenced by the physical appearance of trial participants. In one study (Fontaine & Kiger, 1978), participants watched different versions of a videotaped reenactment of a murder trial. They saw the defendant dressed either in prison clothes or street clothes, and sitting either next to a guard or next to his attorney. Except for these variations, all participants saw the same trial. Results revealed that when the defendant was either wearing prison clothes or sitting next to a guard, he was more likely to be convicted than when he was wearing street clothes or sitting next to his attorney.

How does this relate to the experience of jurors in the Menendez trial? Thornton notes that during the deliberations, jurors discussed the fact that the defendants wore sweaters as opposed to suits to court and that Leslie Abramson often engaged in maternal behavior when interacting with Erik, but they recognized that this may have been a ploy to elicit juror sympathy (December 17). Regardless of their interpretations of the defendants' style of dress and Abramson's behavior, it remains important that jurors noticed these things that were clearly peripheral to the evidence. In addition, Thornton remarks in a letter to her friend Jane that the jurors were "held captive in the courtroom," and that they particularly noticed things that a nonjuror might not notice, such as "a snide remark by one of the attorneys, a subtle reprimand by the judge, a glance exchanged by the defendants, a third or fourth reference to something that has evidently been ruled off-limits" (October 25). Not only are these subtleties not often noticed by nonjurors, they are also not evidence, and therefore should not be assigned any significance by the jurors. However, it is difficult, if not impossible, for someone to ignore or fail to be influenced by information provided by *any* avenue.

Media Coverage

The last, but certainly not least, form of nonevidence to be discussed here is media coverage of the trial, which may influence potential jurors prior to the trial and may continue to influence actual jurors during the trial. Most empirical research done in this area examines the effect of pretrial publicity on verdicts. For example, Moran and Cutler (1991) surveyed jury-eligible people about two highly publicized cases in Florida. They found that the better informed respondents were about the cases, the more they tended to believe that the government had a strong case against the defendants. In addition, they found no relationship between the extent of a respondent's knowledge about the case and that respondent's perceptions of his or her ability to be an impartial juror. In other words, respondents who had been exposed to more information were more likely to believe the defendant was guilty, but did not perceive themselves as biased. This finding is important because prospective jurors who have been exposed to information about the case are often asked whether they can be impartial in spite of that exposure. The research suggests that they may not be able to answer that question accurately.

Once the jury has been selected for a high-profile case, the jurors are admonished by the judge to avoid any media coverage of the case. This is probably easier said than done. Radio and television talk show hosts often make comments (or more accurately, wisecracks) about controversial cases, and even if jurors conscientiously try to avoid news broadcasts and publications, they may be exposed, at least briefly, to media coverage of the case that they are hearing. Thornton's diary gives us some insight into what a juror considers harmful media exposure and the extent to which jurors can avoid such exposure. Consider the following examples:

August 18: Thornton reports accidentally seeing a TV "sound bite" that "corroborated my suspicion that the judge is biased against the defense."

August 28: Thornton sees a TV show featuring children whose parents had pushed them to win at tennis. This is not technically information regarding the case, but could it have had prejudicial effects on jurors?

September 6–10: Thornton remarks that although she has not heard anything that she feels has impaired her objectivity, it is hard to avoid hearing comments about the case on TV and radio. As examples, she mentions hearing one talk show asking callers whether they believed the brothers' abuse story and accepted it as a motive for murder, the host of another talk show suggesting that a few harsh words from one's father did not justify killing him, and the guest on a third describing the Menendez boys as "consummate liars." Thornton always turned these programs off as soon as she became aware of their subject matter.

November 27: Thornton discovers she receives the cable channel Court TV, which was covering the Menendez trial

along with several others, making it difficult to tape for view-
ing after the trial.

December 16: While listening to talk radio, Thornton hears
part of an astrologer's prediction about whether Erik and Lyle
would have a good Christmas.

Obviously, Thornton was exposed to media coverage of the
trial. But was she exposed to so much coverage that she could not
continue to evaluate the evidence objectively? Was the coverage
all inherently damaging, or was there some information that, although relevant to the case (e.g., the brothers' horoscopes), was
not likely to influence her judgment? How does a juror decide
what should be avoided? At one point, Thornton was struggling
with some of these same questions, so she wrote a note to the
judge describing her media exposure. When he did not respond,
she concluded that he did not have a problem with her exposure
(August 2). She also notes that others were probably having similar experiences, indicating that this may actually be the norm for
jurors serving on a high-profile case.

ASSUMPTION 3: JURORS REMEMBER AND COMPREHEND THE EVIDENCE AND INSTRUCTIONS

The legal system assures that jurors can understand and retain all
important information—even in trials such as the Menendez case
that last for months and months. A seemingly endless mass of
isolated facts must be assimilated and comprehended. At first
thought, the fact that there are twelve information processors
would seem to aid in the overall information processing, but during deliberations jurors often disagree as to what actually occurred at the trial. And while a jury may request that a portion of
the trial transcript be read to them, the judge may refuse to do so.
Most judges do not allow jurors to take notes, apparently
fearing that this renders them less able to pay attention to some
of the testimony and gives undue advantage during deliberations

to those who had chosen to take notes (Urbom, 1982). Fortunately, in this trial, as in all California trials, the jury was allowed to take notes, thus facilitating information retention. They were, however, admonished by Judge Weisberg to pay attention.

Psychological research has attempted to evaluate the effects of jurors' note-taking. In a study of jurors in Wisconsin, Heuer and Penrod (1988) found that jurors who were allowed to take notes were more satisfied with their participation than those who were not. More importantly for our purposes, no evidence emerged that those jurors who had taken notes were more influential during deliberations than those who had declined. Thornton makes little reference to note-taking, other than observing that it was allowed and that she and some others did so (September 18). She does not record that any problems arose during deliberations from the decision to permit note-taking.

A second aspect of this assumption is more critical. The judge's instructions to the jury deal with a number of topics, such as the verdict options and the definitions of the charges, including what elements must have been present for a particular crime to have occurred. The judge also gives instructions about which side has the burden of proof and the standard by which the evidence is to be weighed. In a criminal trial such as this, the jurors must be convinced beyond a reasonable doubt that the defendant is guilty before they vote to convict.

Judges' instructions to jurors are fraught with problems. Definitions are usually not specific or operational; for example, the concept of "reasonable doubt" is difficult to interpret. While it is generally taken to mean that the jurors should be strongly convinced but not necessarily completely convinced, individual jurors can differ in how stringent or lax they perceive this standard to be.

Furthermore, most instructions from judges are written in complex legal terminology, with little concern for their comprehension by the layperson. Empirical studies found that jurors usually have poor comprehension of the judge's instructions and that this lack of understanding impaired the accuracy of verdicts (Charrow & Charrow, 1979; Elwork, Sales, & Alfini, 1982).

To make matters even worse, judges typically provide no assistance when juries have problems understanding their instructions. Analyzing the court records of 405 criminal and civil jury trials in the state of Washington, Severance and Loftus (1982) found that a fourth of the juries interrupted their deliberations to request some clarification or amplification of the judges' instructions, but that almost all of the judges refused to embellish or even paraphrase what they had previously provided. Instead, they told their jury to reread the instructions. Indeed, Thornton reports having had this exact experience (January 16).

The fault here lies more with the instructions than with the jurors: "the problem is not jury comprehension, but the comprehensibility of judges' instructions" (Kassin & Wrightsman, 1988, p. 149). Experiments with revised instructions suggest that they do not have to be esoteric or inaccessible to the layperson; instead, in most cases, "the language of the law exceeds in complexity the concepts it is intended to convey" (ibid.).

Ambiguous instructions increase the likelihood that each juror will interpret them idiosyncratically. The problem is compounded when the instructions are given at the end of the trial, as they were in this case. If we assume that jurors have difficulty in suspending judgment fully, this procedure—although it is customary—causes them to play the game before they know its rules.

Thornton's diary entries during deliberations reflect her assessment that some of the jurors did not properly understand the instructions. For example, she wrote on December 17 that "the guys seem to think we were here for the defense to prove there was sexual abuse. They don't apparently understand that the 'burden of proof' is on the prosecution."

It appears that the unspecified definition of "beyond a reasonable doubt" generated differences of opinion and discussion, as Thornton recorded; "I offered that I couldn't be absolutely sure that Erik was sexually abused, but that I don't have to be absolutely sure for it to raise a 'reasonable doubt' in my mind as to the degree of Erik's guilt" (December 17). A few days later she commented that since it's Erik on trial, all we have to do is decide if we have a reasonable doubt or not—it's up to the prosecution to *prove* there was a plan to kill. Yes, this is basically the same speech I gave last week, but it doesn't seem to be sinking in" (December 20).

Some of the confusion over burden of proof in this case may stem from the type of defense used. In most criminal cases, the prosecution's duty is to prove that the defendant performed some wrongful act. However, Lyle and Erik Menendez came into the trial admitting that they had shot their parents. Hence, the prosecutor's responsibility became, in effect, to prove the *reason* that the brothers killed their parents—in essence, to prove beyond a reasonable doubt that they had *not* acted in self-defense. In the minds of some jurors, accustomed to a system in which prosecutors simply must prove "who did it," the burden in such a case may be shifted (regardless of what the law actually says) to the defense, which must provide evidence that the defendants were justified in their actions.

ASSUMPTION 4: JURORS CAN SUSPEND JUDGMENT

In addition to admonishing the Menendez jurors to avoid all information about the case outside of the courtroom, the judge instructed them not to make any final opinions until they had heard all the evidence and had received his instructions on the law. This is a reflection of a fourth assumption regarding jurors made by our legal system: they have the ability to suspend judgment in a case until all evidence has been presented. As psychologists, we must again argue that this requirement is extremely difficult, if not impossible, to follow. The possible influence of an attorney's opening statements has been discussed: in spite of honest attempts to remain open-minded, jurors *are* persuaded at least somewhat by opening statements. Consider the following example, cited in Kassin and Wrightsman (1988):

> Two young lawyers in a Miami trial, having completed only their opening statements, disagreed over a point of law. The judge asked the jury to leave the courtroom while the issue was resolved. When the jury was summoned back, just a few minutes later, the foreman [in all seriousness] announced, "We've arrived at a verdict, Your Honor" (p. 105).

While most juries would probably not go so far as the Miami jury, people in all situations are motivated to make sense of their world and thus tend to interpret new information from the standpoint of existing opinions. This is not to say that jurors will necessarily draw any final conclusions during the first part of the trial, but they will probably tend to lean in one direction or the other, which will influence how they interpret future information. This tendency was demonstrated by Asch (1946) when he had subjects read a list of words describing a hypothetical person and then indicate how much they liked that person. All subjects read the same list of adjectives, except that half read that the individual was intelligent, industrious, impulsive, critical, stubborn, and envious, while the other half read those same words in the reverse order. Because both groups had read the same adjectives, they should not have differed in the extent to which they liked the individual described. However, Asch found that those who had read the positive adjectives first (i.e., intelligent and industrious) rated the person as significantly more likeable than those who had read the positive descriptors at the end of the list. The information presented first colored the way in which later information was interpreted.

Results of further social psychological research support and extend Asch's findings. For example, Snyder and Swann (1978) had pairs of college students who did not know each other participate in an experiment in which one was to interview the other.

Before they began, the subject acting as the interviewer was told that the interviewee was either introverted or extroverted, although this information was simply made up by the experimenter. During the interview, subjects who had been told they were interviewing an introverted person asked more introvert-related questions, while those who believed they were interviewing an extrovert asked more extrovert-related questions. It appears that once a person has formed a belief, he or she may in fact search for information to confirm that belief.

In addition to seeking information that confirms our beliefs, we are also likely to cling to those beliefs in spite of disconfirming information. For example, in one study, subjects were provided with information suggesting either that risk takers make better fire fighters or that they make poor fire fighters. They were then asked to develop an explanation for this relationship between risk taking and fire fighting. After generating their reasons, subjects were told that they had been randomly assigned to hear that risk takers make either good or bad fire fighters, and that they were just as likely to have been assigned to the opposite condition. In spite of this disconfirming information, subjects continued to cling to their beliefs about the relationship between risk-taking and fire-fighting ability (Anderson, Lepper, & Ross, 1980; Ross & Anderson, 1980; Ross, Lepper, & Hubbard, 1975).

How does all of this relate to jurors? As mentioned, after listening to opening statements, jurors almost inevitably lean toward one side or the other. Preliminary beliefs that are formed at this stage of the trial will then be likely to lead jurors to seek out information to confirm those beliefs and to discount any arguments that disconfirm the belief. Such bias-confirming behavior is not generally performed consciously but rather is an adaptive information-processing strategy that is for the most part subconscious.

Thornton appears to have been more impressed by the defense's opening statements than the prosecution's. The following entries from her diary suggest that this may have subconsciously influenced the way in which she received and interpreted evidence presented throughout the trial:

> *September 25:* She states that at this point in the trial Lyle appears to be telling the truth, while Dr. Oziel (the prosecution witness) seems to be lying.
>
> *October 14:* She concludes that lifelong psychological maltreatment could have rendered Erik incapable of having planned his parents' murder.
>
> *October 18:* She decides that the defendants may have been convinced that their lives were in imminent danger. (This is the conclusion needed to find the defendants guilty of manslaughter rather than murder.) Thornton also provides counterarguments for the notion that Lyle and Erik may have intentionally planned to make the murder look disorganized.
>
> *November 17:* She writes that, due to the way things have developed during the trial, the "confession" tape actually serves to strengthen the *defense* (see also December 20 and 22).

Again, we must point out that the formation of early opinions does not appear to be easily avoided, and that individuals are generally unaware of their biased processing of later information. However, in considering Thornton's final opinion about the case, it is difficult to weigh the influence of the defense's opening statements and the relative strength of the defense's case against an apparent lack of credible prosecution evidence and/or poor presentation of the prosecution's case.

On several occasions, Thornton presents counterarguments to the prosecution's theories:

> *September 22:* She provides counterarguments to refute the prosecution's attempt to demonstrate that the defendants

were trying to get away with murder by lying about the killings.

September 23: She offers counterarguments to explain why Lyle would have used his calling card to make a local call at a pay phone. (For additional counterarguments, see October 20 and 29.)

This may, but does not necessarily, mean that Thornton reached an early decision. Jurors *should* counterargue the prosecution's evidence, even if there is no defense opening statement, because the prosecution has the burden of proof.

There are also occasions on which she agrees with the prosecution's line of questioning:

September 22: She feels Bozanich is rightfully giving Lyle the third degree.

October 20: She agrees with the prosecution that poor planning is not the same as no planning at all.

November 18: She supports the prosecution's position that the fact that Dr. Oziel is a bad therapist does not mean the brothers did not plan the killings.

Indeed, there are several diary entries that indicate that Thornton made a real effort to keep an open mind:

August 29: She reports that she feels sorry for the defendants and that she can see how they might have been driven to kill their parents. However, she also states that this does not mean that she thinks that they should get away with it.

September 24: She notes that the judge admonished the jury not to form any final opinions until they had heard all of the evidence and states that she was relieved when he said not to make any *final* opinions. This may be her acknowledgment that she was leaning toward the defense side, but also demon-strates her attempt to keep an open mind until all of the evi-dence had been presented.

November 24: She states that if the prosecution does not offer something irrefutable quite soon, she cannot vote that Erik is guilty.

Thornton was clearly making a conscious effort to abide by the rule that jurors not reach any final conclusions until all of the evidence has been presented. However, once a person finds a particular position to be more logical or acceptable, it becomes difficult to put that initial position aside and interpret every new piece of information as if no previous knowledge existed. Asking jurors to do this is like asking a person to read a book and treat each new chapter as if it were the first. This is not possible, nor is it consistent with our everyday information-processing strategies. Just as prior experiences cannot be left at the courthouse doorstep, opinions formed as the trial progresses cannot be cast from the mind, nor should they be, as each witness steps down from the witness stand.

ASSUMPTION 5: JURORS DELIBERATE ON THE EVIDENCE

The courts assume that juries are decision-making groups that generate objective and fact-based outcomes, and generally it is true that jury verdicts are consistent with the weight of the evi-dence (Visher, 1987). But often ignored is the possibility that jury deliberations are subject to the same pressures and emotional be-havior that operate in certain other decision-making groups. In addition, highly publicized trials carry their own unique pressure.

Group Pressure

Social psychologists Deutsch and Gerard (1955) proposed that two types of social influence may operate on members of groups. *Informational* social influence uses facts and logic, and produces conformity because of the persuasiveness of the arguments and the desire of people to be correct in their judgments. In contrast, *normative* social influence employs emotional appeals and leads to a public conformity that is motivated by a fear of appearing deviant. Decision-making groups—especially when unanimity is a requirement—may reject, ridicule, and punish individuals who impede the achievement of agreement by adhering to a deviant position (Schachter, 1951).

Most decision-making groups reflect a combination of informational and normative influence. Juries are no exception. Many years ago Kalven and Zeisel (1966) noted that the deliberation process "is an interesting combination of rational persuasion, sheer social pressure, and the psychological mechanism by which individual perceptions undergo change when exposed to group discussion" (p. 489).

Thornton's diary reveals her awareness, halfway through the trial, of a difference of opinion among the jurors as well as a desire for a unanimous outcome:

October 25: "We may be all wrong, but there is a perception among the women on the jury that the men are not buying the defendant's story. You don't have to 'discuss the case among yourselves' to figure out whether someone is sympathetic or not. Anyway, the men and women appear divided and there are six of each. . . . I am hoping that future evidence and/or the judge's instructions will unite us in a verdict even if there is disagreement on some of the details."

December 2: "I couldn't care less whether or not Erik is gay—it doesn't have anything to do with whether or not he planned to kill his parents, as far as I can tell. However, I have the feeling that to certain jurors it is a big, huge, important factor."

The diary entries reflect the combination of normative and informational social influence operating within the jury:

December 17: Thornton recounts how the group moves from "venting" feelings to "expressing our concerns in a somewhat more civilized manner."

December 20 and 22: She describes that what is logical and persuasive for one juror is given conflicting interpretation by another.

January 3: She refers to jurors yelling and calling each other names, blatant examples of normative social influence.

January 4: She writes, "I lost my temper today and yelled at [another juror], who had interrupted me (among others) one time too many."

January 6: She states, "These guys (I hate to lump them all together after my tirade on Tuesday, but they're all driving me crazy) can't even let us get to our point without jumping in and interrupting for one reason or another."

On even the last day of the jury's deliberations (January 13) one juror was referring to certain others as "ignorant asses."

The American legal system assumes that jury deliberations contain a vigorous exchange of information and a minimum of normative pressure. However, careful reading of the deliberations section of Thornton's diary (December 15–January 13) reveals the contentiousness of the normative influence perspective along with the logical arguments generated as attempts at informational influence. Despite this unpleasant mixture, one goal of the legal system was achieved: jurors did not conform simply as a result of pressure. The split vote that led to a mistrial did accurately reflect the individual jurors' private beliefs.

The Highly Publicized Trial
The Menendez trial was not only heavily publicized—it was televised minute by minute on Court TV. The jurors were told that the camera would not be showing them, and there is no evidence

that they were made self-conscious by its physical presence in the courtroom. However, Thornton's diary shows that the jurors were undoubtedly aware that they were being scrutinized by the media and the world:

> *December 27:* She writes, "We are starting to get paranoid about the press. They hang around like vultures."

> *January 11:* She heard someone on the radio discussing how stupid her jury was because they couldn't "agree on the obvious—that Erik is guilty of murder."

This intense media attention, plus the fact that the jurors in this case were not entirely anonymous, may have actually encouraged the authoritarian personalities on the jury to take a firmer pro-prosecution stand to avoid being considered weak as the whole world watched.

SUMMARY AND CONCLUSIONS

The American legal system seems to idealize trial jurors as characteristically passive and jury deliberation as characteristically reasonable. This diary provides ample evidence to question each of these assumptions.

What seems most clear about Hazel Thornton's performance as a juror is that she is an *active* processor of information throughout the trial. Even before the presentation of evidence, she speculates as to why she was chosen as a juror (July 18). At several points she wonders what the point of particular testimony is (see, for example, July 21), and she continually evaluates the quality of the evidence. She recognizes early on that one of the tasks of the jury is to decide just what is most important (July 22: "I can see we are going to be getting a lot of information, and it is hard to tell now what is going to end up being important."), yet she does not shy away from this responsibility. She reflects an awareness of sources of bias—in fact, a sophistication about the distinction between a witness's appearance and credibility that would surprise attorneys and judges who see jurors as inert receptacles of information. Consider, as an example, her following statement: "The tough thing is that just because you're looking at someone you wouldn't trust as far as you could throw them doesn't mean they're not telling the truth all or part of the time on the stand" (July 26).

Thornton is aware of the dangers of jurors being influenced by outside sources—from the media, friends, and family. She does not exclude such information entirely—she notes it is impossible to do so—but she trusts herself to know when enough is enough. In short, this juror is revealed to be a much more complex person than the stereotyped conception of the uninvolved juror. Should such a revelation be of concern to the legal system? How would a trial judge react to her diary?

It is our position that Thornton is simply being human. She possesses past experiences and perspectives that influence how she reacts to witnesses and evidence. She understands the evidence and the judge's instructions; she conscientiously tries to separate evidence from nonevidence; she monitors her own attitudes; and she worries about jumping to conclusions. She anticipates possible conflicts during the deliberations, and, when these occur, she argues her position logically but also on occasion loses her temper.

So, why was this a hung jury? With so many variables at play, it is impossible to pinpoint the cause. It would be easier and more worthwhile to speculate had there been a lone holdout juror, but the Erik Menendez jurors were evenly and hopelessly divided.

The Menendez brothers are scheduled to be retried. Perhaps a change in players will make all the difference in the outcome of the trial. At this time, Judge Stanley Weisberg and Leslie Abramson (again representing Erik) are the only participants remaining from the first trial; Lyle's defense attorneys and the prosecution team are new. A different panel of jurors will certainly bring with it a new set of backgrounds, personalities, and biases. However, this is still a very controversial, highly publicized case; without effective, preferably attorney-directed voir dire, and/or a reduction in the charges, and/or a change in the quantity and quality of the evidence, it may happen that the next jury will also be a hung jury.

REFERENCES

Adorno, T. W., Frenkel-Brunswik, E., Levinson, D., & Sanford, R. N. (1950). *The authoritarian personality.* New York: Harper and Row.

Anderson, C. A., Lepper, M. R., & Ross, L. (1980). Perseverance of social theories: The role of explanation in the persistence of discredited information. *Journal of Personality and Social Psychology, 39,* 1037–1049.

Asch, S. E. (1946). Forming impressions of personality. *Journal of Abnormal and Social Psychology, 41,* 258–290.

Bower, G. H., Black, J. B., & Turner, T. J. (1979). Scripts in memory for text. *Cognitive Psychology, 37,* 177–220.

Brehm, J. W. (1966). *A theory of psychological reactance.* Orlando, FL: Academic Press.

Brill, S. (1984, December). Inside the DeLorean jury room. *American Lawyer,* pp. 1, 94–105.

Charrow, R. P., & Charrow, V. R. (1979). Making legal language understandable: A psycholinguistic study of jury instructions. *Columbia Law Review, 79,* 1306–1374.

Deutsch, M., & Gerard, H. B. (1955). A story of normative and informational social influence upon individual judgment. *Journal of Abnormal and Social Psychology, 51,* 629–636.

Elwork, A., Sales, B. D., & Alfini, J. J. (1982). *Making jury instructions understandable.* Charlottesville, VA: Michie.

Finnegan, W. (1944, January 31). Doubt. *New Yorker,* pp. 48–67.

Fitzgerald, R., & Ellsworth, P. C. (1984). Due process versus crime control: Death-qualification and jury attitudes. *Law and Human Behavior, 8,* 31–52.

Fontaine, G., & Kiger, R. (1978). The effects of defendant dress and supervision on judgments of simulated jurors: An exploratory study. *Law and Human Behavior, 2,* 63–71.

Garcia, L. T., & Griffitt, W. (1978). Authoritarianism-situation interactions in the determination of punitiveness: Engaging authoritarian ideology. *Journal of Research in Personality, 12,* 469–478.

Gerbasi, K. C., Zuckerman, M., & Reis, H. T. (1977). Justice needs a new blindfold: A review of mock jury research. *Psychological Bulletin, 84,* 323–345.

Hamilton, V. L. (1976). Individual differences in ascriptions of responsibility, guilt, and appropriate punishment. In G. Bermant, C. Nemeth, & N. Vidmar (Eds.), *Psychology and the law* (pp. 239–264). Lexington, MA: Heath.

Hastie, R., Penrod, S. D., & Pennington, N. (1983). *Inside the jury.* Cambridge, MA: Harvard University Press.

Heuer, L., & Penrod, S. (1988). Increasing jurors' participation in trials: A field experiment with jury notetaking and question asking. *Law and Human Behavior, 12,* 231–262.

Jones, S. E. (1987). Judge- versus attorney-conducted voir dire: An empirical investigation of juror candor. *Law and Human Behavior, 11,* 131–146.

Kalven, H., & Zeisel, H. (1966). *The American jury.* Boston: Little, Brown.

Kassin, S. M., & Wrightsman, L. S. (1988). *The American jury on trial.* New York: Hemisphere.

Lerner, M. J. (1970). The desire for justice and reactions to victims. In J. Macaulay & L. Berkowitz (Eds.), *Altruism and helping behavior* (pp. 205–229). Orlando, FL: Academic Press.

Lesly, M. (1988). *Subway gunman: A juror's account of the Bernhard Goetz trial.* Latham, NY: British American.

Marshall, L. L., & Smith, A. (1986). The effects of demand characteristics, evaluation anxiety, and expectancy on juror honesty during voir dire. *Journal of Psychology, 120,* 205–217.

Moran, G., & Cutler, B. L. (1991). The prejudicial impact of pretrial publicity. *Journal of Applied Social Psychology, 21,* 345–367.

Narby, D. J., Cutler, B. L., & Moran, G. (1993). A meta-analysis of the association between authoritarianism and jurors' perception of defendant culpabilities. Unpublished manuscript. Florida International University, Miami.

Phares, E. J., & Wilson, K. G. (1972). Responsibility attribution: Role of outcome severity, situational ambiguity, and internal-external control. *Journal of Personality, 40,* 392–406.

Pyszczynski, T., Greenberg, J., Mack, D., & Wrightsman, L. S. (1981). Opening statements in a jury trial: The effect of promising more than the evidence can show. *Journal of Applied Social Psychology, 11,* 434–444.

Ross, L., & Anderson, C. A. (1980). Shortcomings in the attribution process: On the origins and maintenance of erroneous social assessments. In A. Tversky, D. Kahneman, & P. Slovic (Eds.), *Judgments under uncertainty: Heuristics and biases.* New York: Cambridge University Press.

Ross, L., Lepper, M. R., & Hubbard, M. (1975). Perseverance in self-perception: Biased attributional processes in the debriefing paradigm. *Journal of Personality and Social Psychology, 32,* 880–892.

Roth, M. P. (1986). *The juror and the general.* New York: William Morrow.

Rotter, J. B. (1966). Generalized expectancies for internal versus external control of reinforcement. *Psychological Monographs, 80* (1, Whole No. 609).

Rubin, Z., & Peplau, L. A. (1975). Who believes in a just world? *Journal of Social Issues, 31*(3), 65–90.

Schachter, S. (1951). Deviation, rejection, and communication. *Journal of Abnormal and Social Psychology, 46,* 190–207.

Severance, L. J., & Loftus, E. F. (1982). Improving the ability of jurors to comprehend and apply criminal jury instructions. *Law and Society Review, 17,* 153–197.

Snyder, M., & Swann, W. B. (1978). Hypothesis testing processes in social interaction. *Journal of Personality and Social Psychology, 36,* 1202–1212.

Sue, S., Smith, R. E., & Caldwell, C. (1973). Effects of inadmissible evidence on the decisions of simulated jurors: A moral dilemma. *Journal of Applied Social Psychology, 3,* 345–353.

Thompson, W. C., Cowan, C. L., Ellsworth, P. C., & Harrington, J. C. (1984). Death penalty attitudes and conviction proneness: The translation of attitudes into verdicts. *Law and Human Behavior, 8,* 95–113.

Urbom, W. K. (1982). Toward better treatment of jurors by judges. *Nebraska Law Review, 61,* 409–427.

Vidmar, N., & Ellsworth, P. C. (1974). Public opinion and the death penalty. *Stanford Law Review, 26,* 1245–1270.

Villaseñor, V. (1977). *Jury: The people vs. Juan Corona.* Boston: Little, Brown.

Visher, C. A. (1987). Juror decision making: The importance of evidence. *Law and Human Behavior, 11,* 1–18.

Wolf, S., & Montgomery, D. A. (1977). Effects of inadmissible evidence on the decisions of simulated jurors: A moral dilemma. *Journal of Applied Social Psychology, 7,* 205–219.

LEGAL COMMENTARY ON THE DIARY

Alan W. Scheflin

Trial by jury is about the best of democracy and about the worst of democracy. Jurors in Athens sentenced Socrates to death for religious crimes against the state, but in England jurors went to prison themselves rather than convict the Quaker William Penn. Juries convicted women as witches in Salem, but they resisted witch hunts for communists in Washington. Juries in the American South freed vigilantes who lynched African-Americans, but in the North they sheltered fugitive slaves and the abolitionists who helped them escape. One jury finds the Broadway musical *Hair* to be obscene, another finds Robert Mapplethorpe's photographs to be art. . . . In short, the drama of trial by jury casts ordinary citizens as villains one day, heroes the next, as they struggle to deal justly with the liberties and properties—sometimes even the lives—of their fellow men and women. (Abramson, 1994)

Over the years I have been privileged to address many jurists and other dignitaries from Asia, Europe, the Middle East and Latin America about the American legal system. Nothing fascinates and baffles these officials more than our jury system. "Surely there are better ways to find facts," they argue. "How can you permit lawyers to use persuasive skills, tricks, and tactics to manipulate juries and then trust the results?" It is my task to demonstrate that despite, or perhaps because of, these "imperfections," the jury is the crown jewel of Anglo-American jurisprudence.

The Menendez case is a perfect illustration of their point. I can hear my noble audience saying what the media and many Americans have been saying: Let us understand. Two spoiled rich boys buy shotguns for the purpose of killing their parents. The boys surprise the parents one evening by breaking into a room and shooting them to death as they are watching television and eating ice cream. The boys admit to the killings. Yet, *two* different juries cannot find the boys guilty of a single crime! How does this case convince us of the value of the jury system? How can we take the Menendez case back to our countries and say "Here is why we must have the jury system in our own land"?

The most obvious response is that the Menendez brothers were tried by a jury of their peers and not by government officials. This fact alone is of extraordinary significance. A democratic society resides power in the people; they, in turn, consent to be governed. When ordinary citizens pass judgment on their fellows and on the laws that bind them together, the community develops profound respect for the legal process. In totalitarian countries, the law is imposed by a very few on the great many, who, by virtue of their legal powerlessness, have no say in its application or enforcement. Law may be feared in such countries, but it is not respected. The threat of legal revolution is ever present. In democratic countries, law is imposed by the people on themselves. The people, sitting as jurors, express a community viewpoint on the appropriate application of those laws (Scheflin, 1971).

There are deeper answers, however, to the question of why the Menendez trials should highlight the value of trial by jury. To find these answers, we must take a deeper look at the Menendez case.

FROM "WHO DONE IT" TO "WHY DONE IT"

Most murder trials begin as a "who done it" as the police scurry to find evidence to identify the perpetrator. The O. J. Simpson trial is a fitting example. No human eyewitness appears to have seen the murders of Simpson's ex-wife Nicole Brown Simpson and her friend Ron Goldman. (Nicole's dog did witness the crime, and the attorneys contacted a dog expert in the unsuccessful hope that the dog could be used to identify the killer.) Prosecutors have been forced to attempt to convict Simpson based on circumstantial evidence—his violence towards his ex-wife, his volatile temperament and intense jealousy, his lack of an alibi, and the overwhelming, although controversial, DNA evidence. Defense lawyers in "who done it" cases have two tasks: (1) attack the validity of the circumstantial evidence; and (2) spin numerous theories about *who else* may have committed the murders.

The Menendez case began its life as a "who done it." When Lyle called 911 to report the slaying of his parents and in subsequent interviews with police, reporters and others afterward, he and his brother denied involvement in the killings. Indeed, they even suggested several theories as to who the perpetrators might be, giving the police names of their father's numerous enemies and more than a hint that it might have been a "mob hit."

The whole complexion of the case, as well as the nature of the advocacy needed on behalf of the brothers, was changed by events that transpired long before Hazel Thornton or any other juror was sworn and seated to hear the case. Before the brothers could be brought to trial, California courts had to grapple with the complicated questions raised by the fact that the psychologist, Dr. L. Jerome Oziel, while holding therapy sessions with the brothers, had tape-recorded their confessions. It was not until three years and a week after the killings, on August 27, 1992, that the California Supreme Court issued its ultimate judgment on these issues, allowing the brothers' trials to get underway. An analysis of the factual circumstances and complicated legal questions concerning these volatile tapes is presented in the Appendix to this commentary.

It was the existence of the taped confessions that turned the Menendez trials from "who done it" to "why done it." If the communications made during therapy sessions were to be admissible in court, the brothers could no longer maintain their innocence. As a consequence, the defense lawyers would have to change the nature of their advocacy because it would not be possible to plead the boys as uninvolved orphans. Instead, the defense task necessarily shifted to providing the jurors with an explanation for the brothers' actions—why they were driven to the extreme of slaughtering the parents who had showered them with material wealth and prestige.

ADVOCACY FOR THE DEFENSE

Although the William Kennedy Smith rape trial (Dunne, 1992) had already drawn large audiences to courtroom television, the Menendez case was an even bigger attraction. Americans by the millions sat glued to Court TV to watch the contentious trials unfold as both brothers were tried together, although each had a separate jury. Those with long memories could not help but be reminded of the infamous Leopold and Loeb case from Chicago in 1924 (Higdon, 1975). Two young men with genius IQs from exceptionally wealthy families had killed a teenaged boy. The community demanded their death, but the brilliance of Clarence Darrow saved their lives. Would Leslie Abramson and Jill Lansing, the stellar lead defense attorneys, duplicate one of Darrow's greatest triumphs?

Ironically, Darrow and Abramson had opposite problems. For Darrow, the issue was arousing *any* sympathy at all for his spoiled, privileged clients. For Abramson, the problem involved arousing *too much* sympathy, thereby triggering a backlash supporting strict convictions. At the time of trial, Los Angeles was simmering under the sympathy of the Rodney King jurors, whose failure to convict the police officers responsible for King's video-taped savage beating sent thousands of LA residents on a rampage of rioting, looting, and maiming. The Reginald Denny jury had also failed to convict the thugs who pulled an innocent truck driver from his van and beat him to within an inch of his life. Los Angeles juries were getting a bad reputation. Without juror sympathy, the brothers had no hope. But how could their lawyers arouse such sympathy from a community already stung by an overabundance of it?

To make matters worse, the Menendez brothers found their case in the hands of Judge Stanley Weisberg, the same judge who presided over the Rodney King trial, whose jury verdict had erupted LA into flames. Weisberg was no stranger to cases involving sons killing fathers. Several years earlier, he had been the prosecutor in a high-visibility retrial of a son accused of killing his extremely wealthy father. The facts of that case bear an uncanny resemblance to those of the Menendez case. After the first trial ended in a hung jury, Weisberg prosecuted the second trial. He argued that the killing had been done out of greed, just as the Menendez prosecutors were now contending. The defense argued that the son had been abused by the father and thus had acted in self-defense, just as the Menendez defense now claimed. The jury handed Weisberg a sound defeat by finding the defendant guilty of involuntary manslaughter, the mildest verdict available.

Given the admissibility of the Menendez brothers' confessions on the therapy tapes, the defense was obliged to put the best spin on what had led them to commit so horrible a deed. As defense lawyer Jill Lansing stated in her opening remarks to the jury:

> On August 20, 1989, Lyle and Erik Menendez killed their parents. . . . We're not disputing where it happened, how it happened, who did it. We're not disputing when it happened. The only thing that you are going to have to focus on in this trial is why it happened. (Soble and Johnson, 1994, p. 243)

The horrible deed had to have a horrible story behind it. Either the brothers were completely guilty or something terrible had driven them to it. With the juries riveted on what the terrible story behind the horrible deed could be, the Menendez lawyers were set to begin the well known "blame the victim" defense.

The "Blame The Victim" Defense

The art of criminal defense advocacy has one cardinal rule— attribute responsibility elsewhere. When bad things happen, juries demand accountability. Defense lawyers satisfy this demand by supplying carefully crafted answers to the fundamental question in any case where the defendant is known to have killed the victim—why? When Dan White, a conservative, middle-class member of the San Francisco Board of Supervisors, showed up armed at work one day and assassinated the mayor and a fellow Supervisor, there was never any doubt that he had committed the deed. But why? The absence of an answer from the prosecution, coupled with the now-infamous "Twinkie" defense ("I was on an uncontrollable sugar high"), resulted in avoidance of a murder conviction. White's lawyers painted a pitiful picture of a man stressed to the point of exhaustion, whose voracious intake of junk food pushed him over the edge, thereby providing an answer to the question, "Why did he do it?" (see Weiss, 1984).

The path was already well-trodden when Darrow, in the 1924 Leopold and Loeb case, blamed his clients' wealthy families for their sons' emotionally warped upbringing. Yes, the boys were rich in worldly possessions, Darrow argued, but they were impoverished in emotion, heart, and spirit. The parents had reared them as soulless monsters, and that is how they acted.

Leopold's and Loeb's families were still alive at the time of their trial and could have refuted Darrow's portrayals, but at the cost of sending their sons to death. The modern cases on "blame the victim" have involved more convenient circumstances—the victims are dead.

Richard Herrin repeatedly and savagely hammered the skull

of his girlfriend, Bonnie Garland, as she lay sleeping in her bedroom in her parents' home. She barely lived until found by her family in the morning. At the trial, Jack Litman, Herrin's lawyer, successfully put Bonnie on trial by depicting her as a callous manipulator of Herrin's deep emotional feelings toward her. As Bonnie's parents watched in horrified silence, the community turned its sympathy and affection to the murderer and not his slain victim (Gaylin, 1982; Meyer, 1982).

Fresh from his victory in the Bonnie Garland case, defense attorney Jack Litman once again used the "blame the victim" defense with great success in a case with national publicity—the "Preppy Murder Trial" (Taubman, 1988; Wolfe, 1989). Eighteen-year-old Jennifer Levin's semiclad body was found in New York's Central Park. Her killer was her date, Robert Chambers, Jr., a handsome prep school graduate who confessed to the killing as an unintended accident during an episode of "rough sex." By the time the case was presented to the jury, however, the victim had become the predator, and the killer had become the victim. By all accounts, the defense succeeded in painting a nasty portrait of Jennifer before a plea bargain ended the proceedings.

The "blame the victim" defense reached its zenith in the "Jewish American Princess" case, where thirty-four-year-old Elana Steinberg was stabbed twenty-six times with a kitchen knife by her husband of fifteen years (Frondorf, 1988). At the trial, defense attorney Robert Hirsch meticulously depicted the deceased wife as a nagging, shrewish, carping intimidator who never gave her husband a moment's respite from her ceaseless spending sprees and vitriolic tongue. In short, Hirsch portrayed his client as a man under unremitting stress until he "snapped" during a moment of temporary insanity. Hirsch made sure that his client was dressed simply and conservatively, in contrast to the expensive clothes and jewelry he usually wore. At appropriate moments, the jury observed the defendant sobbing to express his remorse now that he was back to normal. The jury accepted his "temporary insanity" theory, otherwise known as the "nagging defense," and acquitted him of all charges.

As a high-profile defense attorney with experience in sensational murder trials, Leslie Abramson was no stranger to the "blame the victim" defense. Indeed, in an earlier case bearing a remarkable similarity with the Menendez facts, Abramson had won a verdict of voluntary manslaughter, and a sentence of probation, for a seventeen-year-old boy who had brutally murdered his wealthy father. Her defense? The boy was psychologically and physically abused by his father on a repeated basis. During the Menendez case, courtroom observers noticed a connection between the two cases when the boy attended the trial one day.

It would be wrong to conclude that the "blame the victim" defense is always a con game played on gullible jurors. Society has recognized that not all killings are to be treated identically. Some killings are legally justified; others are morally repugnant. In between, the law recognizes a variety of gradations based upon circumstances and motivations. The great jurist Oliver Wendell Holmes, Jr., once remarked that even a dog knows the difference between being accidentally tripped over and deliberately kicked. The circumstances that lead a person to conclude that killing another is his or her best choice are crucial to the moral blameworthiness that must be present in criminal convictions. Battered spouses and abused children have all too often faced juries in homicide cases (Mones, 1991). There may be good reason to treat them differently from those who kill for greed.

LESSONS FROM THE MENENDEZ CASE

What can the Menendez case teach us? Why does it represent what is valuable about the jury system? It is time to answer these questions.

For some, the Menendez trial represents a complete disaster. Pierce O'Donnell, an extraordinarily gifted attorney with many high-visibility cases to his credit, has written critically about the case:

> With the benefit of hindsight, we can now see how an apparent slam-dunk murder prosecution was derailed by carefully rehearsed testimony, brilliant defense advocacy, underfunded prosecutors caught by surprise, a well-meaning but indecisive trial judge, and a group of jurors manipulated to accept an outlandish defense. The resulting mistrial was a miscarriage of justice. (Novelli & Walker, 1995, p. 252)

O'Donnell's emotional frustration at the mistrial resembles the views of Erik's male jurors. No doubt millions share this view (Dershowitz, 1994). It mirrors the perplexity foreign dignitaries express when they ask for justification for the American jury system.

It would be a mistake, however, to draw erroneous conclusions as to what went wrong and no conclusions as to what went right. On this vital subject Hazel Thornton's diary provides a gold mine of valuable insights and lessons. Her observations help steer us away from the simplistic knee-jerk "blame the messenger" attacks on juries, and toward a more socially constructive understanding of the workings of the justice system.

Books by jurors about their experiences are a remarkable resource. For one, they remind us of the uniqueness of each individual. Giraud Chester (1970), in his account of jury service in a murder case, makes the significant point that "the jury was a microcosm of our society, and the jurors displayed attitudes and values that were often at startling variance with stereotypes" (Preface). No matter how clever lawyers believe they have been in picking jurors (see Scheflin, 1990), the fierce independence of every person's unique spirit will continue to be asserted. We cannot be cubbyholed. Chester is also alerting us to the fact that the jury is composed of a variety of members of the community who cannot be expected to think and act alike. We trust juries because they bring a communal judgment, one forged by the tempering of the many viewpoints into the one verdict. While O'Donnell's position represents one aspect of the community's thinking, it does not represent the thinking of the entire community. When he criticizes the failure of the Menendez juries to return a verdict, he really means they failed to return the verdict he would like to have heard. But the jury must speak for the community as a whole.

By reading juror books, such as those written by Villaseñor (1977) on the Juan Corona mass murder trial, by Kennebeck (1973) on a trial of thirteen Black Panther party members, and by Timothy (1974; see Scheflin, 1977) on the Angela Davis trial, one's faith is restored. We see how neighbors and strangers from all walks of life and from diverse backgrounds conscientiously work together to reach a common verdict with which they all can feel satisfied.

Thornton's diary gives us another backstage look at the workings of the jury in processing and deliberating information. What are the lessons it teaches about the Menendez case?

Lesson 1: Improve Prosecution Strategy

Assuming that O'Donnell is correct that the trial went wrong, what should be fixed? O'Donnell's attack, as quoted above, condemns the competence of everyone at the trial except the defendants and their lawyers. If there is one important legal lesson to be learned from the Menendez trial, it must certainly involve the performance of prosecutors in high-visibility cases.

While the Menendez prosecutors unfolded their case for murder in the first degree with admirable skill, they faltered badly when it came time to respond to the defense claims of abuse. As O'Donnell notes:

> If the prosecution miscalculated, it was in not perceiving the cumulative effect on the jury of months of testimony about alleged sexual and mental cruelty, and the like. The prosecution mounted a weak and ineffective rebuttal that largely ig-

nored the main thrust of the defense: the defendants' mental state due to the supposed abuse. In my opinion that was a fatal mistake.

In retrospect, we can see that the jurors were almost brainwashed. . . .

It was a brilliant strategy, flawlessly executed. (Novelli and Walker, 1995, p. 258)

Thornton too took due notice of the instances in which the prosecution failed to prove its case. In describing the increasingly unpleasant nature of the jury deliberations, she observes:

Yes, the jury deliberation process was a battle of the sexes, and the men called us names, but that is not the issue here. The women on Erik's jury were not particularly compassionate or confused or controlled by their emotions. I do think, however, that because they could accept the possibility of a lifetime of abuse leading someone to kill out of fear, and *because the prosecution did not prove to them otherwise,* they were able, according to the law, to give Erik the benefit of their reasonable doubt. (viii) [emphasis in original]

What went wrong with the prosecution? Sadly, the answer must be: many things. One of the great difficulties of a prosecutor's job in a murder case is that the story he or she must tell about how the crime occurred usually has become old news. What is exciting at trial, and what holds media attention, is the *new* story presented by the defense—the excuse, alibi, or justification that is pleaded. Prosecutors must learn to match the emotional theatrics of the defense. The first rule of persuasion is to satisfy the audience—here, the jury.

More importantly, the Menendez prosecutors failed at the most basic task—to counter the opposition's strategy. Once the case became a "why done it," the arguments available to the defense to arouse sympathy were not hard to figure out. Why is it that prosecutors failed to address the defense's only hope for their clients? At the very beginning of the trial, Thornton notes the difference in advocacy:

> Prosecuting attorney Lester Kuriyama didn't have anything surprising to say. His comments were brief and to the point about how cold and calculating and greedy he intended to prove the defendants were. But defense attorney Leslie Abramson spelled it right out, saying, "The question isn't *who* murdered Jose and Mary Menendez, but *why* they were murdered." (July 20)

The extent to which the prosecution failed to capture the attention of the jurors, failed to rebut the abused/battered child defense, and failed to persuade that this was a simple "kill for cash" case, is well illustrated by Thornton throughout her diary. It is right here, at the doorstep of the prosecution, that concern for the breakdown of justice must begin.

Interestingly, though not surprisingly, a careful analysis of the "blame the victim" cases discussed above reveals exactly the same point—prosecutors focused on the *how* of the crime and not sufficiently on the *why* of it. In all of the "blame the victim" cases mentioned, prosecutors napped while defense lawyers touched the heartstrings of merciful jurors. In none of the cases did prosecutors take seriously the idea that the "blame the victim" defense might be successful. This defense often may be the only card in the defense hand, but prosecutors consistently get trumped by it.

Another point about prosecutorial difficulties is noticeable in Thornton's comments. Once it was clear that information from the tapes would be admitted, the prosecution built its case around Dr. Oziel, the star witness for conviction. But Oziel, constantly in ethical difficulty with his profession and facing lawsuits for improper sexual behavior, mind control, and other unsavory charges, was a poor candidate for the spotlight. His character lent credence to the defense argument that he was using the tapes to manipulate the brothers and using their alleged threat to manipulate Judalon Smyth. Thornton probably reflects most courtroom observers' judgment when she referred to him as "Dr. Weasel" (August 11). Yet, despite Oziel's thorough lack of credibility, Thornton reminds herself that "the tough thing is that because you're looking at someone you wouldn't trust as far as you could throw them doesn't mean they're not telling the truth all or part of the time on the stand" (July 26).

The defense "star" witness was clearly Lyle. Perceived as the stronger and more dangerous of the two brothers, his testimony could make or break the case. By all accounts, Lyle was tremendously effective. Thornton notes that "either that boy is the best actor I've ever seen in my life or he's telling the utter truth. . . . Either way, he held up extremely well under X-exam, in my opinion" (September 25). At another point she writes that "all I gotta say is that, if he is lying, someone really did their homework on the subject of child abuse" (September 10). Most observers are in agreement (Novelli and Walker, 1995; Davis, 1994; Soble and Johnson, 1994).

In the battle between believing Oziel or Lyle, Lyle was the clear victor, unless one took the stance "a pox on both their houses." Dominick Dunne, who had written one major unfavorable piece on the Menendez brothers before the trial (Dunne, 1990), wrote an even more unflattering piece as the trial was ending (Dunne, 1993). Dunne frankly states, "I feel not an ounce of sympathy for these two young killers, even though I acknowledge that they lived a miserable life with a pitiful mother and a detestable father" (ibid., p. 256). At another point he writes: "There is not a single sympathetic character in the Menendez story. There is no one to root for. This is as lousy a bunch of human beings as you could find" (ibid., p. 312). Yet, after watching Lyle on the stand, Dunne, although unpersuaded himself, acknowledged that it was a spectacular performance that gripped the courtroom audience and the jurors: "He created a model for future defense witnesses to emulate" (Dunne, 1994, p. 111).

Thornton also contrasted the two "star" witnesses: "The

thing is, both stories, Oziel's and Lyle's, are plausible. Certainly not all the facts are in yet, but so far it comes down to this for me: Lyle appears to be telling the truth and Oziel appears to be a liar" (September 25).

Once it became clear, as Thornton has noted, that the prosecution was not undermining the abused/battered child defense, and was relying on the testimony of a psychologist who had committed ethical violations and whose character was disreputable, there was a good reason for the jurors to believe the defense was telling the truth. In effect, the jurors heard only one side of the case. They were not "brainwashed"; they simply heard half of a whole conversation.

When O'Donnell talks about having a "slam-dunk" case, he replicates the most commonly made prosecutorial error—failure to give credence to the arguments that will be raised by the defense. Overconfidence by the prosecution is the major reason for their underestimation of the potential persuasiveness of the defense position. O'Donnell bemoans the fact that "lay jurors do not neatly compartmentalize evidence like lawyers and judges" (Novelli & Walker, 1995, p. 258). It is for that very reason that we have juries, and not trial by attorney and judge alone. As the U.S. Supreme Court noted in *Duncan v. Louisiana* (1968), the jury in criminal cases acts as the "conscience of the community," a role that requires heart as well as mind.

Lesson 2: Value Merciful Juries

It is worth remembering that *every juror* in the Menendez case voted to *convict* the brothers of two homicide offenses. Neither jury thought that the brothers' past should excuse the killings. Approximately half the jurors either did not believe the brothers' stories of sexual abuse or found the stories insufficient reason to reduce the charge from murder in the first degree. The other half believed that the stories of abuse made it plausible that the killings had been committed out of fear, thereby reducing the charge from murder to manslaughter, as the judge instructed.

One point that is quite crucial in Thornton's diary is her continuing insistence on the burden of proof. Jurors who chose manslaughter over murder were not convinced beyond a reasonable doubt that the abuse allegations were false. For these jurors, the prosecution had failed to provide the necessary evidence to answer the question, "Are you sure beyond a reasonable doubt that the abuse did not occur and that the brothers were not fearful of harm to themselves from their parents?" Note that it is not necessary to *believe* the brothers. Indeed, some jurors could *disbelieve* them and yet vote for manslaughter on the grounds that the prosecution had not removed all reasonable doubts. There is that possibility that the brothers were telling the truth. As long as it exists, there is reasonable doubt.

It may be that some jurors acted as what I have previously called "merciful jurors" (Scheflin & Van Dyke, 1980 and 1991). Upon occasion, juries are called upon to make very difficult choices. These choices are not about facts, although factual disputes may exist in a case. The toughest choices juries must make always involve disputable matters of policy, politics, or morality. In these cases, morality and law may conflict, forcing jurors to choose between justice and law. Cases of euthanasia, civil disobedience, abortion protest, and the like may appear to force jurors to pit their legal duty against their moral conscience. Whether choices are made in favor of strictness or leniency, jurors will be criticized.

When jurors have opted for leniency, they have been criticized for being weak and gullible. But mercy is a vital part of human nature. Michael Musmanno, a former justice of the Pennsylvania Supreme Court, was a brilliant lawyer who won his first 42 cases and 60 of his first 64 cases. In writing about why he had been so successful, Musmanno emphasized his awareness of the softer side of people. As he shrewdly observed:

> More people "feel" their way than think their way through life. The basic emotions can never be obliterated or sub-

merged, and to ignore them in a speech to the jury is to display an unawareness of reality; for every case is a slice of raw life boiled, broiled, and roasted over the fires which generate from the friction and clash between human hates and human loves. (Musmanno, 1958, p. 244)

In a sense, half the Menendez jurors voted to be merciful. In a system that mandates proof beyond a reasonable doubt, these jurors gave the brothers the benefit of the doubt. There is much to be praised about living in a world of "merciful" jurors rather than one where jurors are vengeful.

Lesson 3: Eliminate Child Abuse
Why were jurors sympathetic and merciful in the Menendez case? In large part because of the childhood sexual abuse in the Menendez family. The Menendez hung juries tell us that our society has great compassion and concern about childhood sexual abuse. Most experts admit that programs presently existing to help children are inadequate, poorly funded, and often unsuccessful.

In the 1950s, the popular TV show "I Love Lucy" was prohibited from using the word "pregnant." Lucy had to say she was "with child" or "expecting." In that repressed climate, frank talk about child abuse was unthinkable. Times and mores have changed. Today, even the most conservative statistics about child abuse are alarming (see Kalichman, 1993). Also alarming is the fact that this violence against children often breeds children who are even more violent. The upwardly spiraling cycle of violence threatens the safety and depletes the resources of the community. It should come as no surprise that a large portion of our prison population, especially those inmates on death row, suffered abuse as children. Is it not time to heed the silent voices of the children in pain?

Lesson 4: Appreciate Elegant Advocacy
In every profession, and every occupation, there are individuals who perform as virtuosos. These masters of their craft give the rest of us an inspirational peek at perfection. Musicians, athletes,

and actors are evaluated on this scale, and so too are lawyers. Oddly enough, law schools generally do not teach artistry. Of the dozens of books to be read in the dozens of law courses to be taken, students will almost never read a single passage about the techniques of great lawyers. While some students may have heard of some of the great lawyers in the past and present, they will be unfamiliar with what, in fact, made them great. While advocacy is taught in law schools, the art of advocacy generally is not.

Lawyers must be persuaders, yet only one law school in the country teaches persuasion. When people hire lawyers they expect to receive well trained, skilled professionals—and rightfully so. Lawyers must be especially excellent at the work they do because, as with doctors, human life may hang in the balance. The lawyer is the client's fiduciary, warrior, and champion.

The Menendez case gave us a glimpse at how criminal defense should be conducted. From the decisions made, to their ultimate execution, the defense was virtually flawless. While the prosecution made predictable mistakes, the defense made wise choices. The advocacy on both sides should be studied by students, because there is much to be learned from it.

It is perhaps rather morbid to observe that the test of great advocacy is to be found with the more hopeless cases. The greater the evidence against the client, the more heinous the crime, and the more unpleasant the defendant, the greater the test of an advocate's skills. It may appear that lawyers are attracted, with ghoulish glee, to hopeless cases and hopeless clients. This image is part of the broader notion that lawyers are deceivers whose function it is to manipulate jurors and judges.

This perception is unfair and unfortunate. Doctors too are tested by the more hopeless cases, because this is where the greatest learning takes place. The lawyer has essentially one job—to make the client's case as reasonable, as attractive, and as persuasive as possible. Within the rules of ethics and evidence, the lawyer must help others to see the client in the most sympathetic light.

In order for a lawyer to help others see the client favorably, the lawyer must in the process help them to learn something about themselves. You cannot feel for another person without feeling something about yourself. In this sense, lawyers perform an underutilized public service—they help the community to become alert to dangers, responsive to problems, caring about misfortunes, and responsive to needed social change.

The Menendez case teaches us much about advocacy. And the advocacy teaches us much about ourselves.

CONCLUSION

At one point, Hazel Thornton says "Jury duty is like eavesdropping for a living" (October 25). Well, with her diary we get to eavesdrop on an eavesdropper. We are treated to the fascination of watching her mind processing the information, moving gradually from deliberation to conclusion. There are also valuable insights for trial lawyers on techniques that work and do not work on jurors.

One of the most significant aspects of Thornton's diary is the depiction of the deliberation process when the jurors finally began to discuss the evidence. The thoroughness with which that jury considered each alternative and the breadth of discussion about how to interpret the evidence are truly impressive. The Menendez juries worked very hard to persuade to unanimity. Given the effort put forth by these jurors—all of them—the community might be disappointed by their failure to reach a verdict, but cannot fault the sincerity, dedication, and commitment they brought to the task.

APPENDIX: THE PSYCHOTHERAPY PRIVILEGE

The legal question that converted the Menendez case from a "who done it" to a "why done it" involved the protection given to therapy patients that permits them to reveal their deepest secrets without fear of public disclosure. Some states do not offer such confidentiality protection to patients. For example, in *State v. Beatty*, a significant Missouri case decided in 1989, a woman confessed to her therapist that she had robbed a store. The therapist anonymously called Crime Stoppers and provided sufficient information for his patient to be arrested by the police. The Missouri Court of Appeals held that because the legislature had not specifically enacted a statute to protect confidences of patients, no such protection was available, despite the fact that the disclosure violated the ethical rules of the therapist's profession. Missouri law was rapidly changed by the legislature after this case.

Most states do protect confidences by statutes that label these confidences as "privileged" from public discovery. Information that is privileged cannot be obtained by court order and must not be revealed voluntarily by the person to whom the confidence was given.

The oldest privilege recognized by law is the attorney-client privilege, which dates back at least five centuries. One of the more recent is the psychotherapist-patient privilege, which was derived from the venerable physician-patient privilege. The psychotherapist-patient privilege has been created in the last few decades by legislatures in some states, while others regulate therapists under the broader physician-patient privilege. Both privileges recognize that what a person tells a therapist is confidential and privileged, even if what the therapist hears is a confession of murder. The therapist cannot be compelled in court to reveal the confession, and the law requires that the therapist outside the courtroom must protect and preserve its secrecy. The protection of privileged information is so important that even if the therapist violates the law and reveals the confession, the confession is still inadmissible in court.

The psychotherapist-patient privilege only applies, however, when the information is confidential, and the privilege itself is not absolute. There are several exceptions that *permit* the therapist to disclose otherwise confidential information, and several major exceptions that *require* it. In the latter category is the mandatory reporting of the sexual abuse of children and the abuse of elders.

One of the most controversial questions concerning the privilege is whether it should apply to seal the lips of a therapist if the patient has revealed an intent to do serious harm to a third person. Suppose a psychologist hears a patient threaten to kill a specific person and believes the patient will carry out the threat. An absolute privilege would prevent the therapist from warning the intended victim to seek protection.

Attorneys face the same ethical issue with dangerous clients who threaten to maim or kill adverse witnesses. A San Diego County Bar Association opinion in 1990 adopted an absolute privilege by telling lawyers that their ethical duty is to maintain silence, even though failure to warn is likely to result in the death of a person. As for therapists caught in this dilemma, however, California law reaches a different conclusion. California statutes specifically recognize a psychotherapist-patient privilege that gives the patient the right to prevent disclosure of confidential communications uttered during the therapy sessions (California Evidence Code § 1014). The legislature made it clear that this privilege was necessary in order to encourage dangerous persons to seek psychotherapy without fear that what they said to the therapist would later be disclosed in a criminal proceeding.

Legislation in California, and many other states, recognizes a "dangerous patient" exception to the psychotherapist-patient privilege that *permits* disclosure of otherwise confidential information when the therapist reasonably believes that (1) the patient will carry out the threat; and (2) the disclosure of certain information is necessary to prevent the harm (California Evidence Code § 1024).

In 1976, California became the first state to *require* therapists to warn third persons of the threats made against them by the therapist's dangerous patient and to make them civilly liable if they do not. This obligation was created by the California Supreme Court in the famous *Tarasoff* case, the facts of which are simple and sad. A young man entered a counseling session at a university clinic. He told the psychologist that he intended to kill Tatiana Tarasoff, a young woman who had spurned his advances. The psychologist, believing that the threat would be carried out, called the campus police and suggested emergency involuntary commitment. The police detained the young man briefly, then released him, believing he was rational. (Note the irony of the psychologist making the law enforcement decision that he should be committed, while the police made the psychiatric decision that he was sane!). The young man soon thereafter killed Tatiana. The California Supreme Court held that the psychologist had had a duty to protect the young woman by notifying her directly of the potential threat to her life. Several years later, the California legislature passed a statute accepting this duty (California Civil Code § 43.92).

While the *Tarasoff* opinion was very clear about imposing a duty to protect threatened third parties, it was silent about what happens to the information revealed by the therapist. If the therapist has already revealed confidential information to the intended victim, can the police and prosecutors have access to what was said in the therapy sessions? The answer to this crucial question was unclear in California when the Menendez brothers confessed to Dr. Oziel and threatened that they might have to kill him as well.

It should be noted that the brothers have denied making the threats. If their claim is true, and if Oziel was unreasonable in feeling threatened, the brothers would be entitled to suppress from evidence not only the contents of the therapy sessions, but also the information conveyed to Oziel's wife and to his mistress Judalon Smyth. The brothers claimed that Oziel was unreasonable in feeling threatened because he was manipulating them in order to obtain some control over their millions and manipulating Smyth by scaring her into believing that if she did not follow his orders, the brothers would kill her. These factual issues were not relevant to the resolution of the legal issue as posed by the courts, which was based on the assumption that the brothers had threatened Oziel. If they had, do the police and prosecutors have access to the contents of the therapy sessions? Naturally, if the threats had not been made, the legal issue would be irrelevant, because the police and prosecutors would have no exception to the privilege to cite as a justification for the confidential information. For the rest of this discussion of the legal issues, it will be assumed that the threats were made and that Oziel was reasonable in feeling threatened.

The Menendez brothers might never have been caught were it not for their foolish act of threatening Oziel. When Erik originally confessed to Oziel, that confession was privileged. The prosecution would not be entitled to obtain disclosure of what had been said in therapy. It was Lyle's threats, joined by Erik's, that became their undoing. Their crucial mistake was making a threat against their therapist, which he believed they would carry out. Once they had crossed this verbal line, California law provided the prosecution with an entry into the information discussed at the therapy sessions.

What was unknown in law at the time Lyle and Erik made their threats was the vital issue of how big an entry the prosecution might be granted. For example, could the prosecution be entitled to learn (1) everything discussed in the sessions; (2) everything the brothers said that led Oziel to feel threatened; or (3) only statements Oziel actually made when he warned his wife and mistress?

The Menendez brothers made a compelling argument in favor of the nondisclosure of the contents of the therapy tapes. "What we said in those sessions," they in essence argued, "should remain privileged, because the purpose of the *Tarasoff* duty and the 'dangerous patient' exception is to allow some confidences to be revealed, but only where the disclosure is *necessary* for the *preven-*

tion of the harm. Now that the crime has been committed, the harm obviously cannot be prevented, and so disclosure of what was said in therapy and by Oziel to others is impermissible."

The prosecution had seized, but was not permitted without court order to hear, tapes of four therapy sessions with Oziel in which the brothers discussed their crime. The prosecution suspected that the information on the tapes had not been disclosed to anyone other than Oziel and that the information would be proof that the brothers had premeditated the crimes. Could any or all four be admitted into evidence?

The Four Therapy Sessions

October 31, 1989
It was at this crucial therapy session that Erik confessed to Oziel that the brothers had killed their parents. Oziel, believing that Lyle was the more dangerous brother, asked that Erik bring Lyle into the session. While they were waiting, Oziel explained to his girlfriend, Judalon Smyth, that "if I let [Erik] tell Lyle, and I'm not there to see Lyle's face, to see the psychology of what's going on with Lyle, I'm really afraid for you and my kids and myself" (*People v. Menendez*, 1991). When Lyle arrived, Oziel felt that his fears were justified. Lyle was furious that his brother had talked. Oziel claimed that, in his presence, Lyle said to Erik:

> I can't believe you did this! I can't believe you told him! I don't even have a brother now! I could get rid of you for this! Now I hope you know what we are going to do. I hope you realize what we are going to have to do. We've got to kill him and anyone associated to him. (ibid.)

If Oziel is to be believed, it was at this moment, with Lyle's initial threat to Oziel, that the brothers made the crucial mistake that cracked open the "perfect crime." The confession of a past crime is absolutely privileged. Without the threat, Oziel's lips were sealed.

After the session, Oziel warned his wife to take the kids and leave town, and he warned Judalon Smyth to protect herself. As part of these warnings, Oziel described the confessions and his belief that the brothers were very dangerous. Oziel decided that his best survival strategy was to convince the brothers that he was their ally and that he could testify as to the cruelty of their childhood. He later stated to Lyle that the continuation of the therapy sessions would look like the brothers had remorse for what they had done and were getting help. Tape 1 is the audiotape Oziel made based on his notes about this explosive session.

November 2, 1989
Oziel informed the brothers that if they threatened him again, their threats would not be confidential, and that if he were harmed, duplicate tapes he made describing the October 31 session would be sent to the police. Lyle laughed and confirmed that the brothers had considered killing Oziel, but were concerned that it would not look good if people associated with the brothers were murdered. Lyle also said that it would be wise for Oziel to tape the sessions, because then he could introduce information that might mitigate the severity of the crime. The brothers then discussed their motivation for the murders, which was not greed but rather a desire to be free from their father's domination and ridicule.

After the session, Oziel felt that although the threats uttered during the October 31 session were still real, the brothers were less likely to carry them out. His fears returned, however, when he discovered that the brothers had lied to him about a vacation they said they were about to take. Oziel reaffirmed the dangers to his wife and to Smyth. Tape 2 is an audio recording of Oziel's notes concerning this session.

November 28, 1989
Erik saw Oziel alone, without Lyle. Erik said that he thought that Lyle did not want more therapy because "I don't think he wants to be controlled by anybody . . . that's why he murdered my

parents. . . . He just wants to be free and he wants to do whatever he wants to do. He doesn't want anybody bugging him too much" (ibid.). Lyle would return to the therapy sessions, Erik noted, in order to "strategize" about the killings. Erik also admitted to a fear that Lyle might kill him as well.

After the session, Oziel still believed that the brothers might kill him. He decided to try to convince them to disclose the killings to their attorney. Even though that communication would be protected from disclosure under the attorney-client privilege, Oziel reasoned that the more people who knew about the crime, the less likely all of them would be killed. Tape 3 is an audio recording of Oziel's notes about the session.

December 11, 1989
Earlier in the month, the brothers had confessed to their attorney. Oziel felt that this disclosure to the attorney lessened the threat of violence. At this session, Lyle and Erik discussed their feelings about each other and everyone in the family. Tape 4 is an audio recording of a portion of the actual therapy session. It is the most controversial of the tapes because it is the only one where the brothers actually speak. The other tapes contained Oziel's notes on the sessions and were therefore subject to the argument that he had, for his own personal motives, misrepresented or misreported what had occurred.

Oziel claimed that he never lost his fear that the brothers might make good on their threats. When the police seized the tapes in March 1990, several months after the last therapy session, Oziel asked for police protection based on the threats contained in the tapes.

THE COURTS AND THE TAPES

The law governing the protection given to confidential information disclosed in therapy sessions changed every year in California from 1989, when the Menendez killings took place, to 1992, when the brothers' trial began. Ironically, the case that finally settled the law was the California Supreme Court's decision on the Menendez brothers' legal challenge to disclosure of the tapes.

The Law in 1989

Only a handful of California cases, and none from the California Supreme Court, addressed the discovery of information from therapy sessions. At the time the Menendez brothers committed the killings, California Court of Appeals had decided that if the therapist had already warned the victim and the victim was dead at the time of the trial, whatever had been said to the victim lost its confidential status and could be disclosed, *provided* that what had been told to the victim was *necessary* to avoid the harm. Only statements necessary to avert the crime are permitted to be disclosed to the victim.

Thus, whatever Oziel said to himself, his wife, and Judalon Smyth that was necessary to convey the danger to them could be presented to the jury. But the brothers had a strong legal argument to make: the only *necessary* things to tell the potential victim are the following facts: (1) the caller is a mental health professional; (2) the patient's name; (3) the patient has expressed the intent to do violence to the potential victim; (4) any specific details of timing, method, etc., that would enable the potential victim to escape; and (5) the caller's professional judgment that the patient is likely to act on his or her expressed threat. If the brothers could get a court rule limiting prosecutorial access to just this information, the confessions would remain privileged. No California court has ever held that the mental health professional must disclose *why* the threat was made, or other information about the patient.

The Law in 1990

In 1990, the California Supreme Court held in *People v. Clark*, a case decided one month after the police learned of the existence of Oziel's tapes, that therapy records lose their privilege because of the *Tarasoff* disclosure duty. In essence, the court said that once otherwise confidential information is released to the victim, the entire privilege is lost.

When the Menendez brothers first argued to the Superior Court judge that the tapes should be privileged, the Supreme Court ruling in *Clark* a few months earlier predicted the outcome. The trial judge held that the prosecution could play all four tapes to the jury.

The Law in 1991

The Menendez brothers appealed the trial judge's ruling to the Court of Appeals, which issued its decision on March 28, 1991. The Court of Appeals, which also relied on *Clark*, agreed with the trial judge and concluded that all four tapes could be played to the jury. Interestingly, the court held that the last two tapes were not subject to the privilege because they had been arranged by Oziel to protect himself and were therefore not for the purpose of therapy.

One month after the Court of Appeals decision, the California Supreme Court decided *People v. Wharton*. Two therapists had warned the potential victim of the threat against her by her live-in boyfriend. The warning went unheeded and the threat was carried out. At trial, the prosecutors wanted the therapists to testify about what the defendant had said in therapy that led them to provide the warning. The prosecutors hoped this information would prove the premeditation necessary for a murder conviction. The California Supreme Court decided the case under a special exception to the psychotherapist-patient privilege known as the "dangerous patient" exception (Evidence Code § 1024). This exception permits, but does not require, therapists to provide a warning to persons threatened by their patients. The court said that once the "dangerous patient" exception applies, the prosecutor can compel the therapist to testify concerning (1) the substance of the warning given to the victim; and (2) the defendant's statements given in therapy that "triggered" the warning.

While there had been no real controversy about the therapist testifying about the warning, the holding that discovery could also include what the patient told the therapist gave prosecutors the largest scope possible in obtaining confidential information. *Wharton* was a devastating blow to the Menendez brothers' hopes to keep from the prosecution much of what they had said to Oziel.

Because the Court of Appeals had not had the benefit of the *Wharton* case, and because the California Supreme Court justices were still not pleased that they had properly answered the confidentiality issue, the Supreme Court agreed to hear the Menendez brothers' plea that the tapes be protected as privileged. Ironically, the Menendez case ultimately became the one to settle California law on the complex question of the scope of the psychotherapist-patient privilege and to settle it in favor of broad protection of therapy secrets. Thanks to the Menendez brothers, therapy patients in California now enjoy more privacy than they have in the past.

The Law in 1992
People v. Menendez, decided on August 27, 1992, ended three years of erroneous and confused legal decisions, and it gave the brothers a half-victory by substantially altering the *Wharton* position.

The California Supreme Court upheld the prosecutor's right to hear the October 31 and November 2 tapes, holding that Oziel had reasonable cause to believe that the brothers would carry out their threat. Thus, under the "dangerous patient" exception, this information, which had already been released to the potential victims, was not privileged. Unfortunately, the Supreme Court did not deal with the argument, stated above, that only the patient's name and the threat lose their privileged status, but not the "why" of the threat. The court's opinion appears to permit whatever Oziel said to be introduced into evidence and not just the bare minimum of what it was necessary for him to say. Lawyers in later cases will no doubt pursue this important point.

As to the remaining two tapes, however, the court ruled that they were to be protected because Oziel did not, at that time, have a reasonable belief that the brothers were still dangerous. Thus, the Menendez brothers provided the test case through which the court clarified California law by favoring the protection of confidential information. By virtue of the *Menendez* holding, prosecutors will have less access to therapy tapes than they have enjoyed.

Once the Supreme Court opened the door for the admission of the two tapes dealing with the confessions, the defense strategy was forced to undergo a dramatic shift from a "who done it" to a "why done it."

Generations of lawyers and law students will learn about the Menendez case from the California Supreme Court opinion that gave the brothers a substantial victory by allowing them to prevent the introduction into evidence of two of the tapes, especially the crucial December 11 tape that contains their own voices. In fact, however, the brothers ultimately did not succeed in excluding these two tapes. Because they had made an issue of their mental state and psychological condition at the time of the crime, Judge Weisberg, late in the trial, ruled that the brothers had waived their right to exclude the tapes. Both juries would get to hear the brothers actually speaking to Oziel in therapy.

Once the defense attorneys realized that the introduction of the tapes was inevitable, they fought for and won the right to present the tapes first, before the prosecution. For years, the defense lawyers had fought to keep the tapes out. Now they were back in court to fight for the right to offer the tapes into evidence. The judge's ruling in their favor gave the defense lawyers the opportunity to put an initial, but vital, spin on how to interpret the significance of the tapes. The juries got to hear the tapes in the context of evidence that Oziel had manipulated the sessions for his own self-interest.

The final irony of the case is found in Hazel Thornton's diary. The prosecution, because it thought that the explosive and revealing December 11 tape would cinch a murder conviction, fought relentlessly to get it into evidence. Meanwhile, the defense, believing the tape was terribly damaging for the brothers, fought hard to keep it out. As Thornton's diary informs us, however, many of the jurors felt exactly the opposite. In their view, the tape proved Oziel to be an unconscionable manipulator and thus aroused some sympathy for the brothers.

In the years to come, as lawyers and others look back on the Menendez case, two points will be of major importance. The first involves the outstanding quality of the advocacy on both sides. While the prosecutors were excellent and swayed half the jurors, the defense was virtually flawless. Even skilled advocates can learn a lesson or two by studying this extraordinary case.

The second point concerns the legal precedent set by the California Supreme Court opinion. For many years, in California and elsewhere, this opinion will be cited, argued, and contested in courts and legislatures. The Menendez brothers, and the precedent their case has set, will be studied and debated by future generations of lawyers and therapists.

LEGAL CHRONOLOGY

August 20, 1989
Erik and Lyle kill their parents Jose and Kitty Menendez.

October 31, 1989
Erik confesses the killings to Dr. Oziel during a therapy session. Lyle threatens Oziel. Oziel warns his wife and Judalon Smyth. (Tape 1).

November 2, 1989
Therapy session (Tape 2)

November 28, 1989
Therapy session (Tape 3)

December 11, 1989
Therapy session (Tape 4)

March 5, 1990
Judalon Smyth tells police about the therapy tapes.

March 7, 1990
Search warrant issued for the tapes.

March 8, 1990
Police seize the therapy tapes.

March 12, 1990
Felony complaints filed against the Menendez brothers, who are
both already in jail.

April 5, 1990
California Supreme Court decision in *People v. Clark*

June–August, 1990
Hearings in the California Superior Court on whether the information on the tapes is either (1) privileged; or (2) admissible into
evidence.

August 6, 1990
Superior Court judge rules all four tapes are admissible.

March 28, 1991
California Court of Appeals decision in *People v. Menendez.*

April 29, 1991
California Supreme Court decision in *People v. Wharton*

August 27, 1992
California Supreme Court decision in *People v. Menendez*

July 20, 1993
Menendez trial begins.

January 13, 1994
Erik's jury returns after 106 hours of deliberation.

January 25, 1994
Lyle's jury returns after 139 hours of deliberation.

REFERENCES

Abramson, Jeffrey. 1994. *We, The Jury.* New York: Basic Books.

Chester, Giraud. 1970. *The Ninth Juror.* New York: Random House.

Davis, Don. 1994. *Bad Blood.* New York: St. Martin's Press.

Dershowitz, Alan M. 1994. *The Abuse Excuse.* Boston: Little, Brown and Company.

Dunne, Dominick. 1994. "Menendez Justice." *Vanity Fair,* March, p. 108.

———. 1993. "Dominick Dunne's Courtroom Notebook: The Menendez Murder Trial." *Vanity Fair,* October, p. 252.

———. 1992. "The Verdict." *Vanity Fair,* March, p. 233.

———. 1990. "Nightmare on Elm Drive." *Vanity Fair,* October, p. 198.

Finstad, Suzanne, 1987. *Ulterior Motives.* New York: William Morrow and Company, Inc.

Frondorf, Shirley. 1988. *Death of a "Jewish American Princess."* New York: Berkeley Books.

Gaylin, Willard. 1982. *The Killing of Bonnie Garland.* New York: Penguin Books.

Higdon, Hal. 1975. *The Crime of the Century: The Leopold and Loeb Case.* New York: G. P. Putnam's Sons.

Kalichman, Seth C. 1993. *Mandated Reporting of Suspected Child Abuse: Ethics, Law, and Policy.* Washington, DC: American Psychological Association.

Kennebeck, Edwin. 1973. *Juror Number Four.* New York: W. W. Norton & Company, Inc.

Meyer, Peter. 1982. *The Yale Murder.* New York: Berkeley Books.

Mones, Paul. 1991. *When a Child Kills: Abused Children Who Kill Their Parents.* New York: Pocket Books.

Musmanno, Michael A. 1958. *Verdict*. Garden City, NY: Doubleday & Company, Inc.

Novelli, Norma, and Walker, Mike. 1995. *The Private Diary of Lyle Menendez: In His Own Words*. Beverly Hills: Dove Books.

San Diego County Bar Association. 1990. "Opinions of the Ethics Committee: Ethics Opinion 1990-1."

Scheflin, Alan W. 1990. Book Review [Starr and McCormick, *Jury Selection*]. *Santa Clara University Law Review* 31: 299–306.

———. 1977. Book Review [Ginger, *Jury Selection in Criminal Trials*, and Timothy, *Jury Woman*]. *Santa Clara University Law Review* 17: 247–65.

———. 1971. "Jury Nullification: The Right to Say No." *University of Southern California Law Review* 45: 168–226.

Scheflin, Alan W., and Van Dyke, Jon. 1991. "Merciful Juries: The Resilience of Jury Nullification." *Washington and Lee Law Review* 48: 165–83.

———. 1980. "Jury Nullification: The Contours of a Controversy." *Law and Contemporary Problems* 43: 51–115.

Soble, Ron, and Johnson, John. 1994. *Blood Brothers*. New York: Onyx Books.

Taubman, Bryna. 1988. *The Preppy Murder Trial*. New York: St. Martin's Press.

Timothy, Mary. 1974. *Jury Woman*. Palo Alto, CA: Emty Press.

Villaseñor, Victor. 1977. *Jury: The People v. Juan Corona*. Boston: Little, Brown and Company.

Weiss, Mike. 1984. *Double Play: The San Francisco City Hall Killings*. Reading, MA: Addison-Wesley Publishing Company.

Wolfe, Linda. 1989. *Wasted: The Preppie Murder*. New York: Simon and Schuster.

Legal Cases

Duncan v. Louisiana, 391 U.S. 145 (1968).

People v. Clark, 50 Cal. 3d 583, 268 Cal. Rptr. 399, 789 P.2d 127 (1990).

People v. Menendez, 3 Cal. 4th 435, 11 Cal. Rptr. 2d 92, 834 P.2d 786 (1992).

People v. Menendez, 228 Cal. App. 3d 1320, 279 Cal. Rptr. 571 (2nd Dist. App.) (1991).

People v. Wharton, 53 Cal. 3d 522, 280 Cal. Rptr. 631, 809 P.2d 290 (1991).

State v. Beatty, 770 S.W.2d 387 (Mo. App.) (1989).

Tarasoff v. Regents of University of California, 17 Cal. 3d 425, 131 Cal. Rptr. 14, 551 P.2d 334 (1976).

About the Author and Commentators

Hazel Thornton is a Senior Engineer at Pacific Bell in Pasadena, California. She received her B.S. in mechanical engineering from San Diego State University and her A.S. in drafting and A.A. in fine arts from MiraCosta College in Oceanside. This was her first experience as a juror.

Lawrence S. Wrightsman (Ph.D., University of Minnesota, 1959) is Professor of Psychology at the University of Kansas, Lawrence. He is an author or editor of eighteen books, including *Psychology and the Legal System* (1991), *American Jury on Trial* (1988), and *Confessions in the Courtroom* (1993). He has been doing research on legal processes for almost twenty years and is director of the Kansas Jury Project. He has testified as an expert witness on the accuracy of eyewitness identification, and he has assisted defense attorneys in jury selection in various types of trials ranging from criminal murder cases to civil malpractice suits.

Amy J. Posey received her Ph.D. in social psychology from the University of Kansas at Lawrence and is now Assistant Professor of Psychology at Benedictine College in Atchinson, Kansas. She completed an internship with the Federal Pretrial Services in the Western District of Missouri. She has taught a course in psychology and law, and conducts research on such topics as eyewitness identification and the effects of attorney gender on jury decisions.

Alan W. Scheflin, Professor of Law at Santa Clara University Law School, holds a J.D. from the George Washington University Law School (1966), an LL.M. from the Harvard Law School (1967), and an M.A. in counseling psychology from Santa Clara University (1987). Scheflin's publications include *The Mind Manipulators* (1978), *Trance on Trial* (1989), and *Memory, Therapy, and the Law* (in press). In 1993, Scheflin received the Irving I. Sector Award in honor of his service to the American Society of Clinical Hypnosis. He has been recognized as an expert on mind and behavior control and on suggestion and suggestibility. He teaches the only course on persuasion offered at a law school. Scheflin's fifth book, *Persuasion and Advocacy,* will be completed in 1996.

Index

Abrahamson, Alan, xi
Abramson, Jeffrey, 131, 162
Abramson, Leslie: admonition
  from judge, 16; agrees to represent Erik, 62; article in *People*
  magazine, 40; attacked by Kuriyama, 70; and "blame the victim" defense, 138; closing arguments by, 67–70; in elevator
  with Thornton, 16; extracting
  testimony from Erik, 34, 35, 36;
  goal for Erik, 70; interaction
  with Thornton after the trial, 92;
  media attention toward, 34;
  opening statement by, 8; in second trial, 126; task of, 134;
  Thornton's evaluation of, 8, 16,
  20, 34, 35, 36, 63, 92, 109, 110
"Abuse excuse" debate, vii
Adorno, T. W., 105, 127
Advocacy in criminal defense:
  courses in law schools on, 147;
  effectiveness in Menendez trials,
  147, 148, 160; goals of, 136

Alfini, J. J., 115, 127
Anderson, C. A., 119, 127, 129
Anderson, Fred, 12, 14, 23, 45, 60
Assumptions about juries: empirical findings on, 103; on juror
  bias, 101, 103–108; on jurors'
  focus on evidence, 101–102,
  108–114, 122–125; on jurors'
  remembering evidence, 102,
  114–117; on jurors' suspending
  judgment, 102, 116, 117–122;
  on jury deliberations, 102–103,
  122–125; in the legal system,
  101, 124, 125; Thornton's journal in relation to, 101
Authoritarianism, 105–106, 108,
  125

Battered Woman's Syndrome, 19
Belief in a just world, 105
"Billionaire Boys Club," 13, 79,
  111
Black, J. B., 109, 127